Adding Video to Create an Interactive Filmstrip

p. 86

"It was easy for me to imagine how a filmstrip would make the site more fun and engaging—and I hadn't seen such a thing before."

—Andreas Heim

Creating an Information Display System

p. 122

"My main developmental goal is to facilitate the creation of a hardware and software solution that allows information to travel infinite distance over zero time."

—Todd Marks

Controlling Your Text with CSS

p. 94

"Wouldn't it be great if Flash allowed us to use existing CSS files to format the text in Flash? Well, that's exactly what Flash MX 2004 does!"

—Michelangelo Capraro and Duncan McAlester

JSFL: Using Flash's New Automation Language to Create Text Effects

p. 132

"JSFL is probably the most exciting new feature in Flash MX 2004, and it's certainly the feature we were both most excited about when we got our hands on the new version."

—Michelangelo Capraro and Duncan McAlester

Extending Video in Flash

p. 106

"In creating this project, I wanted to develop a simple, straightforward interface that integrates video into the experience."

—James Williamson

Developing Interfaces for for Pocket PCs

p. 150

"It's my passion to make functional interfaces that are artistic in nature."

—Bill Spencer

Macromedia®

Flash™ MX 2004 Magic

Michelangelo Capraro and Duncan McAlester
with Chad Corbin, DallaVilla Design, Aria Danika,
Andreas Heim, Robert Hoekman, Jr., Todd Marks,
Bill Spencer, and James Williamson

The photograph of the street scene on the cover of this book was taken in New York City by photographer Ed Holub. Playing off of the theme of "flashes of light," which started with the cover image of the first *Magic* book ever—*Macromedia Flash 4 Magic*—this image was chosen for its eye-catching depth. Particularly striking is the way its neon sign and city lights reflect against a rainy evening.

800 East 96th Street, 3rd Floor, Indianapolis, Indiana 46240
An Imprint of Pearson Education
Boston • Indianapolis • London • Munich • New York • San Francisco

Contents at a Glance

Macromedia® Flash™ MX 2004 Magic

International Standard Book Number: 0-7357-1377-4
Library of Congress Catalog Card Number: 2003111988
Printed in the United States of America
First printing: February, 2004
09 08 07 06 05 04   7 6 5 4 3 2

Interpretation of the printing code: The rightmost double-digit number is the year of the book's printing; the rightmost single-digit number is the number of the book's printing. For example, the printing code 04-1 shows that the first printing of the book occurred in 2004.

Trademarks

Warning and Disclaimer

New Riders would like to thank TechSmith Inc. for providing Camtasia Studio 2.0 for the instructional videos developed by LodeStone Digital, LLC.

Publisher
Stephanie Wall

Production Manager
Gina Kanouse

Senior Acquisitions Editor
Linda Bump Harrison

Senior Development Editor
Jennifer Eberhardt

Senior Project Editor
Kristy Hart

Copy Editor
Karen A. Gill

Indexer
Angie Bess

Composition
Kim Scott

Manufacturing Coordinator
Dan Uhrig

Interior Designer
Alan Clements

Cover Designer
Aren Howell

Media Developer
Jay Payne

Marketing
Scott Cowlin
Tammy Detrich
Hannah Onstad Latham

Publicity Manager
Susan Nixon

Let Us Hear Your Voice

As the reader of this book, you are the most important critic and commentator. We value your opinion and want to know what we're doing right, what we could do better, what areas you'd like to see us publish in, and any other words of wisdom you're willing to pass our way.

As the Senior Development Editor for New Riders Publishing, I welcome your comments. You can fax, email, or write me directly to let me know what you did or didn't like about this book—as well as what we can do to make our books stronger. When you write, please be sure to include this book's title, ISBN, and author, as well as your name and phone or fax number. I will carefully review your comments and share them with the author and editors who worked on the book.

Please note that I cannot help you with technical problems related to the topic of this book, and that due to the high volume of email I receive, I might not be able to reply to every message.

Fax: 317-428-3280

Email: jennifer.eberhardt@peachpit.com

Mail: Jennifer Eberhardt
          Senior Development Editor
          New Riders Publishing
          800 East 96th Street, 3rd Floor
          Indianapolis, IN 46240 USA

About the Authors

Michelangelo Capraro

Michelangelo is a multimedia designer and owner of Tin Lion Creative. He speaks at different events on the topic of multimedia programming, design, and usability and has been designing user interfaces and interaction for more than eight years with clients that include business-to-business firms, operating system companies, software makers, and consumer entertainment giants. He began his career designing multimedia CD-ROMs and moved into entertainment industry website design for movies and television shows. Michelangelo has founded several design groups, as well as his own firms over the years and worked as a user experience designer at Be Inc., and later at PalmSource, Inc., where he managed their user experience group. He is coauthor of the book *Skip Intro: Macromedia Flash Usability and Interface Design* (New Riders Publishing, 2002) and conducts workshops and curriculums on multimedia design.

Acknowledgments: I would like to thank the New Riders team, especially Jennifer and Linda, for putting up with us on this project and cracking the whip when needed! Thanks to Duncan, my coauthor, for being the best teammate and making this possible. Thanks to Karen, for putting up with my lack of sleep and for your love and your support.

Duncan McAlester

Duncan lives at the beach and endeavors to one day be retired; until then, he makes a living doing things that he is still astonished people are willing to pay him for—namely, designing and programming various things through his company, Breathe (www.breathedesign.com). When Duncan isn't creating interactive designs, he can be found teaching interface design at the University of California Irvine Extension, sitting in on life drawing classes at the Art Institute of Southern California (his alma mater), or hosting a very informal Flash user group at the local tavern (stop by and say hi). He also speaks on various topics relating to design, multimedia, and interface design and occasionally finds time to sleep.

About the Authors

Chad Corbin

Chad is an award-winning Flash developer best known for his work on lo9ic.com. Originally educated as a mechanical engineer, Chad turned to web design to satisfy his creative tendencies, turning the one-time hobby into a full-time career. Currently, Chad works for Wall Street On Demand, where he develops Flash applications and financial websites for leading investment firms. When he is not working, Chad can be found riding his bike or playing in the mountains nearby his home in Boulder, Colorado.

Acknowledgments: I'd like to thank Shan for putting up with all of the late nights and long hours of coding, my parents for supporting me in whatever I do, and the Flash community for its generosity, creativity, and wealth of knowledge and ideas.

DallaVilla Design

The core team at DallaVilla Design is (clockwise from left) Chris Dallavilla, Creative Director; Ron Thompson, Art Director; Drew Horton, Copywriter; and Rick Williams, Developer. They are a tightly knit group dedicated to producing innovative, exciting work.

Over the past few years, DVd has produced successful, award-winning projects for the entertainment and fashion industries and companies ranging from small to Fortune 500. The studio operates under the philosophy that by combining great design, captivating storytelling, and cutting edge technology, it can create the next level of interactive experience. Although the team at DallaVilla works hard, it also cherishes the time spent in "team-building sessions." To the uneducated observer, these sessions might look very much like a bunch of guys playing video games, but the team assures us it's much more.

You can check out DVd's portfolio and read more about the individual team members at www.dvdsgn.com.

About the Authors

Aria Danika

Aria is an interactive designer, a senior moderator at Flashkit.com, and a member of the Hypermedia Research Centre in London, where she completed her graduate studies in hypermedia and interactive design. She originally trained as a photographer but turned to interactive media while pursuing a B.A. degree in multimedia and photography at Westminster University in London.

Aria freelanced for various broadcasters in the UK including TV3, VH-1, and Granada and later joined BBCi for five years, where she designed and developed rich media applications and games.

Aria is a contributor to *Flash MX Magic* (New Riders Publishing, 2002), and has written many articles on game design and design for interaction. She is based in Brooklyn, New York, spending her free time skateboarding, beta testing games, shooting short films, and exploring interactivity across different platforms, which has led to a series of sound/video experiments, installations, and web toys designed in Director and Flash. Check out www.openedsource.net.

Acknowledgments: Many thanks to my flatmate, Chris, for the brainstorming sessions, keeping me caffeinated, challenging me to GBA games, and testing mine. Thanks also to the flashkit.com members for making learning so much fun. Andy Cameron, thanks for the inspiration and support. Yoshi, I thank you for sharing my sleeping habits and purring while I am debugging code all night in front of the computer. Many thanks to Linda Bump Harrison and Jennifer Eberhardt at New Riders, for their invaluable feedback and hard work. Finally, my parents, thank you!

Andreas Heim

Andreas is from the small town of Hattenhofen, close to Stuttgart in Germany, a center of German car engineering. Originally intending to become a professional soccer player, Andreas's education took him into the area of media studies and programming. After creating an interactive CD-ROM, his focus shifted from film and video to interactive media. His school required him to do a six-month internship, which brought him to Smashing Ideas, where being a soccer-playing-and-beer-drinking German intern was highly respected. He had so much fun in Seattle that he extended his stay to one year before deciding to stay permanently. Andreas currently works on all kinds of cutting-edge digital-media projects, including bringing Flash to devices, while enjoying his time outside of work snowboarding and playing soccer.

Acknowledgments: Thanks to Troy Parke for the inspiration and design, to the great folks at New Riders for letting me contribute to another book, the team at Smashing Ideas, and Anna Hall for all her support.

About the Authors

Robert Hoekman, Jr.

Robert is a Certified Macromedia Flash MX Designer who has worked with Flash since version 3. He is the Founder and Manager of the Flash and Multimedia Users Group of Arizona (FMUG/AZ), an officially recognized Macromedia User Group (MMUG) with more than 130 members. Robert works as a freelance and contract Flash designer and writer and has developed web and CD-ROM content for audiences ranging from music memorabilia collectors to executives for Fortune 1000 companies. He also currently reviews and edits content for InformIT.com's Flash section and contributes to InformIT's Flash web log.

Acknowledgments: I would like more than anything to thank my best friend and wife, Christine, for sitting me down on a Saturday afternoon to teach me to write HTML, a skill which I somehow very quickly parlayed into a career in New Media design. Without her, I'd still be wondering what I want to be when I grow up.

Todd Marks

Todd is an avid developer, designer, instructor, and author of information display technologies. In 2000, Todd moved from teaching mathematics and computer science in the public sector to VP of Research and Development at digitalorganism. In 2002, he founded MindGrub Technologies, LLC and established an information technologies portal, www.mindgrub.net. In 2003, Todd joined PopeDeFlash as the head of Technology for the Unity Project, www.theunityproject.com.

Todd is a Macromedia Certified Developer, Designer, and Subject Matter Expert. His efforts have earned three Flash Film Festival nominations, Macromedia Site of the Day, two Addy awards, and several educational partnerships. Todd has written and contributed to several books, including *Macromedia Flash MX Video* (APress, 2003), *Foundation Dreamweaver MX* (APress, 2003), *Beginning Dreamweaver MX* (Wrox, 2003), *Advanced PHP for Flash MX* (Wrox, 2003), and *Macromedia Flash MX Components Most Wanted* (APress, 2003).

I'd like to thank Dan DesRosiers, Chrissy Rey, and the rest of the crew at ARINC for the cool FIDS project.

About the Authors

Bill Spencer

Bill is the Founder and CEO of The Unity Project.com (www.theunityproject.com), a collaborative effort with Todd Marks. The project's goal is to bring the best of code and art together. Bill is also the Founder and CEO of Popedeflash.com (www.popedeflash.com), the first Flash community dedicated to 3D. He is a well-known speaker, author, and artist, having spoken at many new media conferences, including the popular FlashForward conference series, as well as the FlashKit conferences in Australia and the U.S. Bill has served as an author and technical reviewer for both New Riders and Friends of Ed. He has appeared in *Shift* magazine, *World and I*, and *Computer Arts*, along with other professional journals and periodicals as both an expert in his field and featured work. His work has been a finalist in the Flash Film Festival. He has served as a beta tester for Macromedia, Adobe, Electric Rain, and Discreet, and has served as a technical advisor for Electric Image in the development of Amorphium Pro. Bill also serves as a senior moderator at FlashKit.com, is a staff member of Flashdevils.com, and serves as a moderator for UltraShock.com.

Acknowledgments: I would like to take the time to thank my wife, Sherri, for all the love and support she provided for this project and all the other crazy projects, conferences, and just plain ol' work that comes my way. Without her support, Pope de Flash would not be. I also need to thank my little dachshund Daisey, for providing me with the nudge to take much-needed breaks and to remember to have fun. That's what this is all about!

James Williamson

James is the Director of Training at Lodestone Digital and has more than nine years of print design, web design, and digital prepress experience. He resides in picturesque Rock Hill, South Carolina, and commutes across the border each day to battle Charlotte traffic. In addition to his work with Lodestone Digital, James is the President of the Charlotte Society of Communicating Arts and a member of the Curriculum Advisory Board for the Art Institute of Charlotte.

James has been a featured speaker at several events, including DevCon and FlashForward. He is proudest of his latest project, Morgan Williamson, born June 26, 2003.

Acknowledgments: First off, thanks to Josh Cavalier for the reviews and advice, and to Linda Bump Harrison, Jennifer Eberhardt, and everyone else at New Riders for the opportunity to work on such a wonderful book. Thanks as well to Diana Johnson of Sorenson Media and Kymberlee Weil of FlashForward. Long overdue thanks to Will Hines for answering my emails all those years ago and getting me started in web design. Last, but not least, thanks to my family for your undying support and to my wife, Holly, and my new daughter, Morgan. Welcome to the world, sweetheart.

About the Technical Reviewers

Developing technically accurate books is a priority at New Riders. We rely on the skills and advice of technical experts to guide the authors in the creation and development of their manuscripts. The following reviewers have provided their input—and we offer our thanks for their hard work and dedication.

Erik Bianchi

Erik has more than six years of experience developing Flash-based games and applications for both Fortune 50 and Fortune 500 companies. Currently, Erik works as a software engineer for Surgical Information Systems, where he is responsible for the design, development, and implementation of one of the product's client-side front-ends. Erik is also an active member of the ever-growing Flash community and has contributed to a number of publications. In his spare time, Erik can be found online playing any one of his favorite multiplayer games or in front of a TV on one of his console systems. You can find out more about Erik at www.erikbianchi.com.

Marcus J. Dickinson

Marcus is a freelance Macromedia developer and corporate trainer in the Toronto area. Many prominent companies in North America have sought his skills. He is actively involved in the Toronto community, as well as online, where he moderates numerous forums. He brings an enthusiasm and excitement to Flash that is hard to match. His personal project, *Diaries of War*, promises to be unique and engaging.

Laura McCabe

Laura is a freelance multimedia designer and developer currently living in Baltimore, Maryland. Her eclectic interests have led to an undergraduate degree in psychology; graduate studies in art, design, and multimedia; and work as a writer, trainer, and editor. She has honed her skills in web design, development, and information architecture while working with clients such as AARP, Hershey, and the FDA. In her spare time, Laura is a photographer and inveterate book junkie.

Bill Perry

Bill is a freelance developer who focuses on application development for smart devices, including Pocket PCs. He maintains www.pocketpcflash.net, a Flash development resource for Pocket PCs, is a member of Team Macromedia, has spoken at conferences, and is co-author of the book *Flash Enabled: Flash Design and Development for Devices* (New Riders Publishing, 2002). Currently, Bill is exploring alternative uses of Flash applications with smart devices in wireless environments. You can reach him at bill@pocketpcflash.net

Table of Contents

Table of Contents

How to Make the Most of This Book

This book has been created with special elements in order to make your experience with the manuscript more productive.

- Each project opens with a statement from the author explaining why he or she chose this particular technique or project to share with you and how it will help you in your work. You'll also get a quick, illustrated overview of the project in the section called "It Works Like This."

- Before you start diving into each project, there are several tasks you need to complete in order to prepare your workspace and files. This is covered in the "Preparing to Work" sections.

- At the end of each project, a section called "Now Try This" suggests other ways to apply the methods you've learned, or ways to adapt the project you've just completed, whether it's building on the project itself or swapping out some functionality.

- In addition to the code listings and exercise files on the accompanying CD-ROM, you'll find videos that clearly demonstrate step by step all the procedures you need to complete in order to create the projects.

Conventions Used in This Book

As you work through the projects, keep in mind the following conventions we've used:

- Project files and folders provided on the accompanying CD appear in the text like this: **bold**.

- Many of the techniques in this book require adding or altering some code. All code is highlighted and identified in the text with a listing number (such as Listing 2.3). To apply the code, you can either enter it yourself or locate the listing on the CD, and then copy and paste it into your project. To copy the code for a project from the CD, go to that project's **Code listings** folder and open the corresponding listing text file. For example, the code file for Listing 2.3 is identified on the CD as **02-03.txt**.

- The ➡ symbol appearing in code indicates that the line of code continues on the next line. If you are entering that code by hand, you should simply type it in as one line, without the continuation symbol.

- Text you are asked to enter into fields or code listings will appear like this: underscored.

- Text that appears inside code listings will appear in a special font, like this: code.

- Commands and keyboard shortcuts for both Windows and Mac are included throughout the projects. The Windows option is listed first, then its Mac equivalent, like this: Ctrl/Cmd+B, which means "Hold down the Control key on Windows and press the B key, or on the Mac, press Command and B."

Enjoy creating the magic!
—The New Riders Staff

PROJECT 1 | Constructing a Site Dynamically

Robert Hoekman, Jr.
is a Certified Macromedia
Flash MX Designer and the
founder of the Flash and
Multimedia Users
Group of Arizona.

Robert Hoekman, Jr.

It used to happen so often that it's the principle reason I switched to a cable Internet connection. I'd hop over to a Flash site and, before it could load, I'd have time to go make a sandwich. It seemed designers everywhere were building sites using one, gigantic .FLA and forgetting all about the users on dial-up connections. Eventually, I decided I wanted to do more work with Flash, and the first thing I did was learn to build sites in a modular way, so that I'd never hear a user equate visiting my site to standing in line at the bank.

Building Flash sites is one of my favorite things to do. Whipping up a few sections of content and stringing it together with preloaders, transitions, and text effects makes for a fun project every single time. I'm always learning, and always trying to get it just right. Getting a solid grip on even the most basic methods makes Flash content more rewarding for my clients, and easier for me to build.

It Works Like This

In this project, you'll turn a folder full of files into a fully functioning, robust site whose modules can be easily updated during and after the development process. Many of the techniques covered here are brand-new and will work only in Flash Player 7. Here are the basic steps of the project:

1   Use label frames as named anchors to set up reference points for the button assets.

2   Load images with a `MovieClipLoader` object.

3   Automate the look of your text by applying CSS to text fields with a `TextField.StyleSheet` object.

4   Use a `LoadVars` object to load an external text file that contains variables used to supply HTML-formatted text to the project.

5   Create Shared library assets for use with later projects.

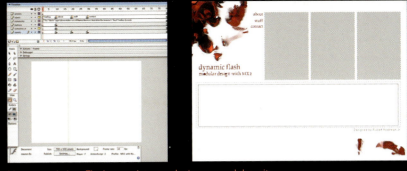

Use an existing Flash template to design a modular site.

Simple tweaks of the original design and underlying code give you a whole new look in less time.

Preparing to Work

To prepare for this project, you will need to do the following:

1   Copy the **Projects/01** folder to your hard drive.

2   Open **index.html** from the **completed_project** folder and click through all three "pages" of the site. Close the browser window when you're finished.

3   Back out of the **completed_project** folder and look through the **01** and **images** folders to become familiar with the files you'll be using.

The **text** and **styles** folders are empty right now. You'll create the files that will go into these folders later on. The **Code listings** folder contains the scripts you will write in this project, so if you would rather not type the scripts, you can import them from the **Code listings** folder.

4   Open **master.fla** from the **01** folder. This is where you'll start.

Note: If you are using Flash MX Professional 2004, choose Window > Project to open the new Project panel, which makes it easy to organize and open all the files for any project.

1   Choose the Create a New Project link and save it as Dynamic_Flash.flp.

2   Use the Add Folder button to create three new folders. Name them text, styles and images. Add the files from the **01** folder on your hard drive to the Project panel, adding images into the images folder. Leave the **text** and **styles** folders in the Project panel empty for now—files will be added here later on—and don't bother making a **widgets** folder.

3   After you've added all the files, right-click/Ctrl-click on **index.html** and choose Make Default Document to specify it as the home page. Don't worry about the Test Project button; you'll get to that later on as well.

Making the Buttons Work

The **master.fla** file will serve as the main interface for your site. At Frame 1, you should see six layers in the Timeline: actions, labels, comments, buttons, container_mc's, and assets. Starting at Frame 10, you can see the graphic symbols that compose the interface. You'll start by setting up the buttons. This part of the lesson has been placed up front to lull you into a false sense of security. (Insert evil laugh here.)

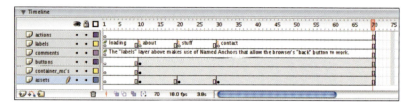

CAUTION

You're going to jump back and forth between frames and layers quite a bit in the next several sections, so be sure you have the correct frame selected before adding code.

Note: Each of the frame labels used in this section is designated as an "anchor" frame in the Property inspector. An anchor frame is a reference point in a movie that a browser can refer back to, so the Back and Forward buttons will work when navigating through a Flash site (Windows only). To take advantage of named anchors, simply choose the Flash with Named Anchors option in the HTML tab of the Publish Settings, and then click the Publish button. If you don't want to use Flash-generated HTML for your site, you can copy and paste the named anchor code, by itself, into your own page or write it yourself.

1   Select the three buttons on the buttons layer at Frame 10, one at a time, and use the Property inspector to give them instance names of about_btn, stuff_btn, and contact_btn, respectively.

2   Select Frame 10 of the actions layer, and then choose Insert > Timeline > Keyframe (F6).

3   Using the Actions panel (Window > Actions, or F9), add this block of code to set up the button behaviors:

Listing 1.1

```
about_btn.onRelease = function() {
    gotoAndStop("about");
};
stuff_btn.onRelease = function() {
    gotoAndStop("stuff");
};
contact_btn.onRelease = function() {
    gotoAndStop("contact");
};
```

Triggered with the onRelease method of the Button object, the about button sends you to the about frame (specified by a frame label on the labels layer) and stops (gotoAndStop). Also, the stuff button jumps to the stuff frame, and so on. Each one of these frames represents a different "page" of the site. Click on any labeled frame and look in the Property inspector to see how this is set up.

The code for the button behaviors should match the following figure:

```
1  about_btn.onRelease = function() {
2      gotoAndStop("about");
3  };
4  stuff_btn.onRelease = function() {
5      gotoAndStop("stuff");
6  };
7  contact_btn.onRelease = function() {
8      gotoAndStop("contact");
9  };
```

4   Save your work.

Using the *MovieClipLoader* Object to Load Assets

Now you'll create an instance of the MovieClipLoader class (Flash Player 7 only). You'll use this object to handle loading most of the images and .swfs in the site. Creating it here will allow you to refer back to it later and use it again.

Note: ActionScript is an Object-Oriented Programming (OOP) language, which essentially means that instances of classes (such as the MovieClip class) can be referred to, and reused, repeatedly, as "objects." For a much better explanation of OOP and other information, check out Webopedia's definition at http://webopedia.com/TERM/o/object_oriented_programming_OOP.html.

1 Select Frame 1 of the actions layer and add this code in the Actions panel:

Listing 1.2

```
stop();
my_mcl = new MovieClipLoader();
my_listener = new Object();
my_listener.onLoadComplete = function(movieClip) {
    trace("Loading is done for "+movieClip);
};
my_ listener.onLoadError = function(movieClip) {
    trace("Error: "+movieClip+" did not load anything.");
    trace("Your load failed for "+movieClip);
};
my_mcl.addListener(my_listener);
```

Here, after instantiating the `MovieClipLoader` object, you also add a "listener" that will access the `onLoadComplete` and `onLoadError` methods of the `MovieClipLoader` object. If something goes wrong during the load process, an error will be reported in the Output panel via the trace commands inside the listener. If all goes well, the message `Loading is done for` *MovieClip name* will appear. The last line of the preceding script simply assigns `my_listener` to `my_mcl`.

2 At Frame 10, note the three gray boxes on the Stage. Select the one on the left. In the Property inspector, give it an instance name of <u>container_1_mc</u>. Then name the other two gray boxes <u>container_2_mc</u> and <u>container_3_mc</u>, from left to right.

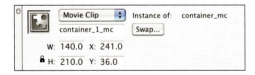

These clips are instances of the `MovieClip` instance called container_mc (which you can find in the Library) and will serve as containers for some external images that you will load in the next step. It is important to note here that external files always load into the top-left corner of a container `MovieClip`, so the gray box inside of container_mc has

been aligned to 0×0 using the Property inspector. If you want to see how this is set up, double-click one of the gray boxes to enter Symbol Editing mode, but be sure to return to Scene 1 before moving on.

Note: Adding `_mc` to the end of `MovieClip` instance names will prompt "code hinting" in the Actions panel. For more information on code hints and code hinting suffixes, see Matthew David's "Naming Conventions" series of blog entries at `www.InformIT.com`. Just go to the Flash section from InformIT's home page, and you'll find the Flash blog. You might have to hunt the archives a little, but it's worth it. While you're there, you might find another familiar name in the blogs (like yours truly).

3 Select Frame 10 of the Actions layer and add this code after the button script that's already there to load images into the corresponding container MovieClips.

Listing 1.3

```
my_mcl.loadClip("images/about1.jpg", "container_1_mc");
my_mcl.loadClip("images/about2.jpg", "container_2_mc");
my_mcl.loadClip("images/red1.jpg", "container_3_mc");
```

This loads some images using the `loadClip` method of the `MovieClipLoader` object.

4 Select Frame 20 of the actions layer (directly above the stuff frame label) and insert a keyframe (F6).

5 In the Actions panel, use this code to call the `MovieClipLoader` once again and load some new images for the "stuff" section:

Listing 1.4

```
my_mcl.loadClip("images/red2.jpg", "container_1_mc");
my_mcl.loadClip("images/stuff1.jpg", "container_2_mc");
my_mcl.loadClip("images/stuff2.jpg", "container_3_mc");
```

Next, you'll use this object one more time to load a form into the "contact" section.

6   Choose File > Open to open **contact.fla**. (Flash MX Professional
    2004 users: Use the Project panel to open this file.) Publish it by
    choosing File > Publish and then close it.

This file has nothing to do with modular design, so the code has
already been added for you. You're off the hook.

7   At Frame 30 of **master.fla**, select the horizontal gray box on the
    Stage (the really long one) and give it the instance name
    container_contact_mc.

8   On Frame 30 of the actions layer (directly above the contact frame
    label), insert a keyframe (F6). Use the loadClip method to load
    contact.swf into container_contact_mc, and again load some new
    images.

Listing 1.5

```
my_mcl.loadClip("contact.swf","container_contact_mc");
my_mcl.loadClip("images/contact1.jpg","container_1_mc");
my_mcl.loadClip("images/contact2.jpg","container_2_mc");
my_mcl.loadClip("images/red3.jpg","container_3_mc");
```

9   Save your work.

Using a *TextField.StyleSheet* Object to Apply CSS

Flash Player 7 now supports the use of Cascading Style Sheets (CSS).
To take advantage of this, you'll create a CSS file, load it with the
TextField.StyleSheet object (Flash Player 7 only), and apply it to two
different text fields.

1   Open your favorite text editor and type this code. I prefer
    Macromedia Dreamweaver for this, but you can use whatever
    you like.

Listing 1.6

```
myStyle {
    font-family: Arial;
    font-size: 12px;
    color: #666666;
}
a:link {
    color: #660000;
}
a:hover {
    color: #666666;
}
```

This CSS code will be applied to text fields in the site.

2   Save this file as myStyle.css in the **styles** folder, and close your text
    editor. (Flash MX Professional 2004 users: Add myStyle.css to the
    styles folder in the Project panel.)

3   Add this code to Frame 1 of the actions layer to create an instance of the `TextField.StyleSheet` class (Flash Player 7). Add it below the code that's already there.

Listing 1.7

```
my_ss = new TextField.StyleSheet();
my_ss.onLoad = function(success) {
    if (success) {
        trace("myStyle.css loaded");
    } else {
        trace("myStyle.css did not load");
    }
};
my_ss.load("styles/myStyle.css");
```

The `Textfield.StyleSheet` instance loads the CSS.

Tip: It's helpful to add a few line breaks between chunks of code because it makes everything easier to read later on, but be aware that if you click the auto-format button in the Actions panel, your line breaks will be lost. To avoid this, add some empty comments between code blocks. Comments can be inserted by typing // at the beginning of a line.

The following figure shows what your code should look like at this point:

```
 +  🔍 ⟡ ⊕ ✔ ≣ (🖗                         ⊛ ℒ 🖹
 1  stop();
 2
 3
 4  my_mcl = new MovieClipLoader();
 5  my_mcl.onLoadComplete = function(movieClip) {
 6     trace("Loading is done for "+movieClip);
 7     var loadProgress = my_mcl.getProgress(movieClip);
 8  };
 9  my_mcl.onLoadError = function(movieClip) {
10     trace("Error: "+movieClip+" did not load anything.");
11     trace("Your load failed for "+movieClip);
12  };
13
14
15  my_ss = new TextField.StyleSheet();
16  my_ss.onLoad = function(success) {
17     if (success) {
18        trace("myStyle.css loaded");
19     } else {
20        trace("myStyle .css did not load");
21     }
22  };
23  my_ss.load("styles/myStyle.css");
```

Be sure that everything is typed exactly the way it is here because ActionScript 2 is strictly case-sensitive. `TextField.StyleSheet` (with capital letters at the beginning of each word) is the name of an ActionScript 2 class, and `textField.styleSheet` (which uses lowercase letters to start the first word before and after the dot) is a *property* of a `TextField` object.

The `onLoad` method is used here to make sure the load goes correctly, and the `trace` commands are used to provide feedback via the Output window. The last line of the script is used to load myStyle.css.

4   At Frame 10, select the dynamic text field on the Stage (indicated by a black dotted line). In the Property inspector, give it an instance name of <u>about_txt</u>. Leave the variable field blank.

5   Still in the Property inspector, next to the menu that says "Multiline," be sure to activate the options for Selectable and Render Text as HTML.

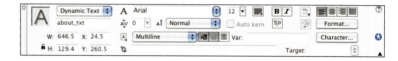

6   On Frame 10 of the actions layer, insert this code to tie the CSS to the about_txt field, and force word wrapping, like so:

Listing 1.8

```
about_txt.wordWrap = true;
about_txt.styleSheet = my_ss;
```

7   Now select the dynamic text field on the Stage at Frame 20. Give it an instance name of <u>stuff_txt</u>, and again activate the options for Selectable and Render Text as HTML in the Property inspector.

8   Finally, select Frame 20 of the actions layer, set up word wrapping, and tie the CSS to the stuff_txt field.

Listing 1.9

```
stuff_txt.wordWrap = true;
stuff_txt.styleSheet = my_ss;
```

9   Save your work.

Using the *LoadVars* Object to Load External Text

Now you'll create an external .txt file that contains two variables and uses an instance of the LoadVars class (Flash Player 6 or higher) to load them and assign them to the text fields. Each variable contains some basic HTML tags that are used to format the text when it appears in the final project.

1   Open your text editor again, and add the following code:

Listing 1.10

```
aboutVar=<b>Need some Flash widgets?</b><br><br><img src=
➡'arrow.swf' width='25' height='15' align='left' hspace=
➡'0' vspace='0'>In the <b>STUFF</b> section of this
➡project, you'll find a couple of Flash widgets you can
➡modify and use in other projects. I've whipped up a
➡contact form and photo slide show just for Flash Magic.
➡Simply copy them from the "widgets" folder on the CD-ROM
➡and modify them as much or as little as you want. Then
➡load them into other Flash projects using the techniques
➡you've learned in this chapter.&
```

All you are doing here is declaring a variable called aboutVar and giving it a value. In this case, its value is a long string of HTML-formatted text. Notice, though, that the block of text here ends with an ampersand (&). When declaring variables in an external file, an ampersand is used to separate the variables. If no ampersand is found, the Flash Player assumes that everything in the .txt file is one variable, so it is important to include it.

2   Because there are two text fields in the site that will display text, you'll create a second variable for the "stuff" section, immediately following the last one. Do not add spaces or line breaks. Just start typing right after the & in the previous variable.

Listing 1.11

```
stuffVar=<b>Get some stuff!</b><br><br><img src='arrow.swf'
➡width='25' height='15' align='left' hspace='0' vspace=
➡'0'>So you <i>do</i> want some Widgets? Great! To get
➡your widgets, just hit the link below and the Widgets
➡folder should come flying right open. If that doesn't
➡work, just look in the folder for this chapter and open
➡it from there.<br><br><img src='arrow.swf' width='25'
➡height='15' align='left' hspace='0' vspace='0'><a href=
➡"widgets/">Show me the Widgets folder!</a>&
```

The following figure shows what your code should look like at this point.

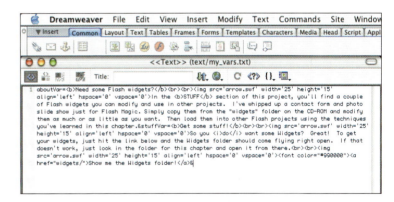

If you've loaded variables into a text field with Flash before (and you're familiar with HTML), you might notice something pretty cool in the previous variables. Flash Player 7 now supports the <img> tag and several of its attributes. You can now load an .swf directly into a text field. In the preceding example, you're doing exactly that. When you are able to contain your excitement, move on.

3   Save this file as <u>my_vars.txt</u> into the **text** folder and close your text editor. (Flash MX Professional 2004 users: Add <u>my_vars.txt</u> to the Project panel, in the **text** folder.)

Note: The additional HTML support in Flash Player 7 means you can now also load .jpg files into text fields. In addition, you can wrap images with <a> tags to turn them into links, and when the movie is published, you can right-click (Windows) or Ctrl-click (Mac) on a link and choose to open it in a new page or copy the link to the Clipboard. Macromedia's work to the `TextField` class has made Flash text much more usable.

---

4   Add this code to Frame 1 of the actions layer. Just add this code beneath everything else so it matches the following image.

Listing 1.12

```
my_lv = new LoadVars();
my_lv.load("text/my_vars.txt");
my_lv.onLoad = function(success) {
  if (success) {
      gotoAndStop("about");
      trace("my_vars.txt loaded correctly");
  } else {
      trace("my_vars.txt did not load.");
  }
};
my_lv.getAbout = function() {
  return this.aboutVar;
};
my_lv.getStuff = function() {
  return this.stuffVar;
};
```

The following figure shows what your code should look like at this point.

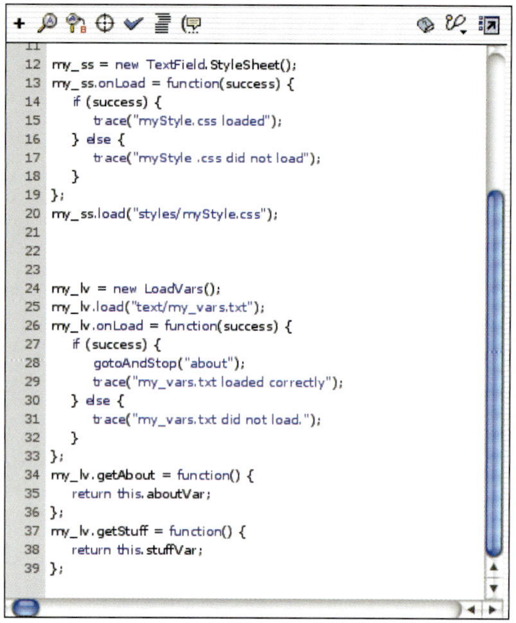

This sets up the `LoadVars` object (Flash Player 6). Here you create an instance of the `LoadVars` class, load my_vars.txt, and store the variables in it for later use.

Several things happen here. First, the `load` method is called to load the .txt file from the **text** folder. If the load is successful, the `onLoad` function sends the playhead to the about frame. If it is not successful, you'll see `my_vars.txt did not load` in the Output window. The `getAbout` and `getStuff` functions retrieve the values of the loaded variables and "hold" them for you via `return` statements.

5   On Frame 10 of the actions layer, add this code to assign the `aboutVar` variable to the text field. Before and after the variable assignment, you'll add tags that apply the loaded CSS to the text.

Listing 1.13

```
about_txt.htmlText = "<myStyle>" + my_lv.aboutVar +
➥ "</myStyle>";
```

6   Finally, select Frame 20 of the actions layer, and send the variable `stuffVar` to the stuff_txt field. Again, you'll wrap the variable in opening and closing tags to apply the CSS to the text field.

Listing 1.14

```
stuff_txt.htmlText = "<myStyle>" + my_lv.stuffVar +
➥ "</myStyle>";
```

The following figure shows what your code should look like at this point. (Line breaks have been addded to the script in the figure to make the code more readable.)

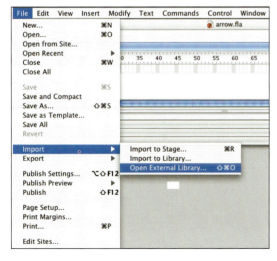

7   Save your work.

Creating a Shared Library Asset

Since Flash MX, you've had the ability to use Shared Libraries, which allow you to load a symbol from the Library of one SWF for use in another movie. Flash MX 2004 allows you to do this three levels deep, and the inception of "policy files" means you can now grab assets from .swf Libraries on other domains. For now, however, you'll keep it simple.

When you created **my_vars.txt** earlier, you added <img> tags to the HTML in both variables, and the image that is called by each variable is arrow.swf. Here, you'll set up the linkage properties of the arrow symbol, pull it into arrow.fla, and then publish the movie so that you can load it into your text fields.

1   Still in master.fla, open the Library (Ctrl/Cmd+L or F11) and locate the graphic symbol called **arrow**.

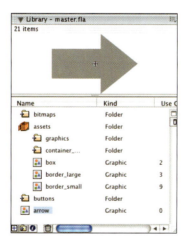

2   Right-click/Ctrl-click on the arrow symbol and select Linkage.

3   In the Identifier field of the resulting dialog box, type <u>arrow</u>. (Seems logical enough, right?)

Under the Linkage section, checkmark Export for ActionScript, Export for Runtime Sharing, and Export in First Frame. This tells the Flash Player to make this symbol available to other movies.

In the URL field, type <u>master.swf</u> to specify the location of the library containing the shared asset.

4   Click OK, save master.fla, and close it. Don't publish it yet; you'll get to that soon. (And it will be very exciting—I swear!)

5   Choose File > Open to open arrow.fla. (Flash MX Professional 2004 users: Use the Project panel to open the file.)

6   Choose File > Import > Open Library for Import, and then locate and choose master.fla.

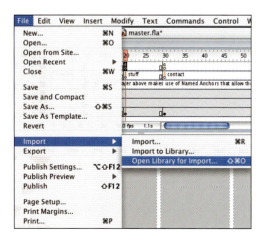

The Library from master.fla should open, and you should now see both libraries. If you don't, press F11.

7   Locate the arrow in the master.fla Library and drag it out to the Stage. Align it to the left edge of the Stage, and center it vertically using the Align panel.

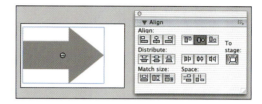

8   Right-click/Ctrl-click on the arrow graphic in the Library for arrow.fla and select Linkage again.

You should see that it has kept its identifier from the original Library, the Linkage section should have Import for runtime sharing checked, and the URL section should still say master.swf. If all that is true, you're in good shape.

Note: Runtime sharing, used here, means you can use symbols from one Flash movie in many other movies without adding file size to any of them. Keep in mind, though, that the Shared Library has to download to the user's computer completely before another .swf can use its assets.

---

9   Save your work, publish the movie (File > Publish) and choose File > Close All to close arrow.fla and the master.fla Library. (Flash MX Professional 2004 users: Add arrow.fla to the Project panel after you close everything.)

When the project is done, several things are going to happen consecutively. First, master.swf is going to load my_vars.txt into a text field. Then, the HTML string inside my_vars.txt will load arrow.swf into the same text field. To really make things confusing, arrow.swf is then going to pull its one and only asset, the arrow symbol, from the master.swf Library and place it on its own Stage. Oddly, the entire process will appear seamless. The only thing you'll actually see is some text with a little arrow next to it. Kinda cool, huh? (I love my job.)

Note: Ultimately, the point is to consolidate the amount of symbols you load in a project. If you have a logo, for example, that you plan to use in several movies throughout a site, turning it into a Shared Library asset will allow you to use the same logo over and over again, in many different movies, without ever having to reload the symbol or add file weight to the project. This makes the user experience much more smooth and efficient. No one will have to wait for the Flash Player to load assets more than once.

Seeing Your Project in Action

There are just two steps left, and you should be feeling the excitement now. If you're not, move on to Project 2, "Creating an Interactive Presentation with Built-In Print Functionality," and forget about this last part. Hey, wait. Don't do that.

1   Open master.fla one last time and choose File > Publish.

Note: Flash MX Professional 2004 users: Now is the moment you've been waiting for. Click the almighty Test Project button. Things might run a bit slow for a minute, but a lot is happening here, so be patient. Soon, your favorite text editor may pop open a copy of index.html for no apparent reason, but don't panic—it means you're done! If you're lucky, index.html will open in a browser. (It depends on what program .html files are associated with on your computer.) If your text editor opens, close the file, and then reopen it in a browser window. If you are not using the Project panel, just choose File > Publish.

You should now see everything you've been hoping for. You should see images load in place of those stodgy gray boxes. You should also see text load into text fields. And you should see a little arrow graphic placed before the text.

Note: If you are missing any of this, go back through the project and make sure you have spelled everything correctly. Spelling mistakes can cause error messages and broken functionality, and more often than not, it can cause your whole project to sit there like a lump looking useless (not that I'm bitter).

2   Finally, click through each page of the site, and be sure to fill out the contact form. The magical Submit button will send your comments directly to my Inbox. Please, no negative comments. I'm sensitive.

If everything is working correctly, pat yourself on the back; you've just learned the techniques that will allow you to create your own Flash site. If you start winning awards, though, please be sure to thank me. If you have questions, I'll be in my office. Contact me at robert@loveandrage.net.

Now Try This

In this project you've learned to use the `MovieClipLoader` and `LoadVars` classes, taken a stab at runtime sharing, and even learned how to apply CSS to Flash text.

Here are some ideas on how to apply the skills you've learned or use the project you've completed in other ways:

- Create a shared Library of photographs and use them in several movies in combination with the photo viewer provided on the accompanying CD.

- Load photographs into `MovieClips` and use CSS to format text fields for captions.

- Use a `MovieClipLoader` object to construct a preloader (arguably, the best use for it) in which the `onLoadProgress` method triggers a progress bar in a `MovieClip`.

- Use the contact form on the accompanying CD (**Projects/02/ widgets/cfmail.cfm**) to process and send email with ColdFusion.

Creating an Interactive Presentation with Built-In Print Functionality

Robert Hoekman, Jr.

Robert Hoekman, Jr.
is a regular contributor of
articles and web logs for the
Flash Reference Guide on
InformIT.com and works as
a technical editor and
author with Lynda.com.

A couple of years ago I was assigned the task of creating a "slideshow presentation" for a trade show, and I knew right away that Flash was the way to go. I'd seen the bored looks on everyone's faces at other events, and I knew that it would take nothing short of a miracle to hold interest. So I got to work, and my client ended up with a project that kept potential customers lined up at the trade show booth for two straight days. It turns out that people appreciate it when you stop boring them to death. Go figure.

It's for this reason that I am excited to show you how a few tweaks and modifications to some existing resources can make your presentation the hit of the party. Bosses love it, clients love it, and you'll be making everyone happy inside of an hour. The point here is that, by respecting your audience, you'll be giving them something to remember—and if they remember you, they'll tell other people. And that's just makes good sense.

It Works Like This

This project is a series of slides that presents content in a linear fashion. The completed presentation includes Back and Forward buttons that trigger the transition from one slide to the next, and a print button in the last slide allows the user to print the entire presentation. Here are the basic steps of the project:

1 Set up the project by deleting unnecessary layers and assets from an existing template.

2 Import new assets from an external library, taking advantage of authortime sharing.

3 Create movieclips to serve as slide transitions.

4 Nest movieclips to create the multiple states of slide transitions.

5 Target the movieclips to play between slides based on user interaction of the Forward and Back buttons.

6 Create a PrintJob object to print the entire presentation, and hide the Forward and Back buttons used in the online presentation.

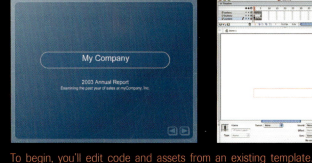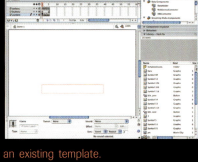

To begin, you'll edit code and assets from an existing template.

You'll end up with a printable slide show.

Preparing to Work

To prepare for this project, you will need to do the following:

1   Copy the **Projects/02** folder from the accompanying CD to your hard drive.

2   Open **FlashVilleTown_complete.swf** and click through the presentation to see what you'll be building. Close it when you're finished.

Setting Up the Template

1   Choose File > New and choose the Templates tab in the New From Template window. Choose Presentations in the Category list, and then choose Tech Presentation from the Templates list. Click OK.

2   Save the file as FlashVilleTown_presentation.fla into the **Projects/02** folder you copied to your hard drive during "Preparing to Work."

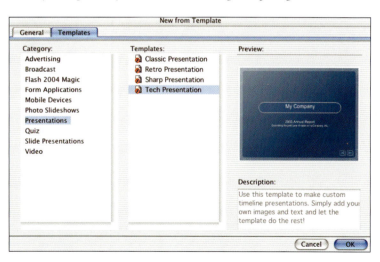

Removing Assets and Layers

As you can see, the template is made up of several layers, a few frames, and some graphics. Almost everything on the Stage will be removed in the next few steps. You're only going to keep the buttons.

1   Remove the following layers by selecting them and clicking the trash can icon in the Timeline: bg purple, bg red orange, bg blue, bg overlay lines, and headers.

The only layers left should be actions, buttons, and content.

2   On the content layer, select Frame 1 and press Backspace/Delete to remove everything on that frame. Do this for each of the remaining four frames.

You should be left with nothing but a white Stage with two pale blue buttons in the bottom-right corner.

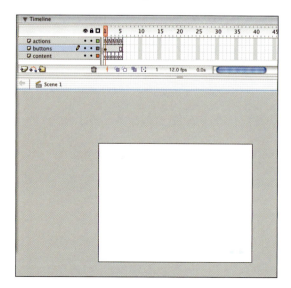

3   Open the Library (Ctrl/Cmd+L) and make sure all the current sym-
    bols are in the **templateAssets** folder. Close the folder by double-
    clicking on it.

Note: Unused symbols in the Library are not exported when you publish an SWF unless you have set up linkage properties for them. For
more about linkage properties, see "Creating a Shared Library Asset"
in Project 1, "Constructing a Site Dynamically."

---

4   On the Stage, double-click the Back button (the arrow pointing to the
    left) to edit the symbol. To make it easier to see, use the Property
    inspector to change the background color of the Stage to black.

5   In the Up frame, or "state," delete the graphic behind the arrow.
    Break the arrow apart by choosing Modify > Break Apart
    (Ctrl/Cmd+B) repeatedly until the arrow appears as a collection of
    dots. Change the color of the arrow to #999999 (light gray) using the
    Property inspector.

6   In the Over state, delete the graphic behind the arrow, break the
    arrow apart, and change its color to #333333.

7   Remove the keyframes in the Down and Hit states by right-
    clicking/Ctrl-clicking on the keyframes and choosing Clear Keyframe
    from the contextual menu.

8   Return to Scene 1 and repeat Steps 4–7 for the Forward button.

9   Return to Scene 1 and change the background color of the Stage back
    to white using the Property inspector.

10   Save your work.

Importing New Assets

Now that you've stripped out the stuff you don't want, it's time to start
building on what's left. Next you're going to get all the new assets together
and lay out the presentation.

1   Choose File > Import > Open External Library and select
    FlashVilleTown_lib.fla from the **02** folder you copied to your hard
    drive in the section "Preparing to Work."

    This Library contains all the assets you'll use for the new presentation.

2   Lock the buttons layer in the Timeline and select Frame 1 of the
    content layer.

3   From the external Library, drag the **bitmaps** folder to the Stage and
    then delete everything. Repeat this for the **buttons**, **new_assets**, and
    slide_content folders.

    Here, you're simply pulling all the contents of the external Library
    into your own Library. (You can also do this by dragging assets straight
    from the external Library to the Library of your new .FLA, without
    putting them on the Stage and deleting them.)

4   Open your own Library (Ctrl/Cmd+L) to make sure the folders transferred properly.

The Stage should still be empty except for the two gray buttons.

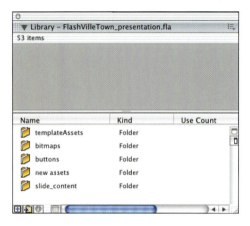

Note: This process is known as *authortime sharing*. The main advantage to this process is that you can create libraries full of graphics that you use often and drag the images into new projects as you need them. In this case, six slides have been laid out for you and converted into symbols. All you have to do is align them on the Stage.

5   Drag **slide_1** from the **slide_content** folder in the Library to the Stage. Place it 17 pixels in from the left edge of the Stage and 108 pixels from the top.

To do this, type the coordinates into the X and Y fields of the Property inspector. X refers to the horizontal position on the Stage, and Y refers to the vertical position.

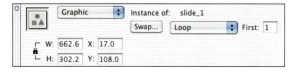

6   Repeat this process for the next five slides, which go on the next five frames of the content layer. Position them at the following coordinates:

slide_2: X = 8, Y = 58
slide_3: X = 18, Y = 34
slide_4: X = 18, Y = 18
slide_5: X = 45, Y = 194
slide_6: X = 230, Y = 35

You will need to insert a keyframe on Frame 6 to add the last slide. To do this, choose Insert > Timeline > Keyframe (F6).

7   You might have noticed that slide_6 is a movie clip. Use the Property inspector to assign it the instance name slide_6_mc.

8   On the buttons layer, insert one frame so that it extends to Frame 6, and then insert a keyframe on Frame 6 of the actions layer.

9   Save your work.

Creating the Animation to Be Used in the Transition

Next you'll create a couple of MovieClips that will provide a visual transition between slides when the presentation is published. Transitions can be a little tricky to construct, so pay close attention to the steps in the next three sections. In this section, you'll create a simple animation that will be used in the transition.

1   Create a new MovieClip (Insert > New Symbol) and call it trans_anim.

2   In Edit mode for trans_anim, drag **blur.png** (in the **bitmaps** folder) from the Library to the Stage. Align the right edge of blur.png to the left of the registration mark (the little + symbol). Zoom out a bit so that you can see everything. Now insert a keyframe on Frame 2.

This is where the animation will start.

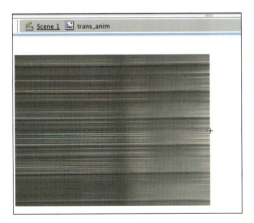

3   Copy and paste the image on Frame 2 so that there are now two copies of it, and position the second image directly to the right of the first image, in a straight line.

4   With the second image selected, choose Modify > Transform > Flip Horizontal.

The two images should now look like a single image. If they don't, move the second image a pixel at a time (using the arrow keys on the keyboard) until it appears seamless and the crosshairs are in the center between the two images.

5   Shift-select the two images, and group them by choosing Modify > Group (Ctrl/Cmd+G).

6   Insert a keyframe on Frame 6.

7   At Frame 6, move the grouped image so that the far right edge is at the left of the registration mark. Press Shift while dragging the image so that it moves in a perfectly straight line.

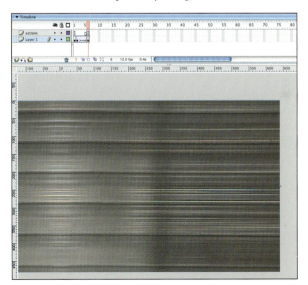

8   Select Frame 2 in the Timeline and choose Motion from the Tween menu in the Property inspector.

This produces an arrow between the two frames in the layer, indicating that it is now a motion tween.

9   Create a new layer and call it <u>actions</u>.

10 On Frame 1 of the actions layer, use the Actions panel (F9) to add a stop command:

Listing 2.1

```
stop();
```

11 On Frame 6 of the actions layer, insert another keyframe and add this code:

Listing 2.2

```
gotoAndPlay(2);
```

The gotoAndPlay() command loops the animation during the transition.

A movie clip that you'll create in a minute will control this animation. The stop() command is added here so that the animation doesn't run the entire time the presentation is open. If this were not added, the animation would loop endlessly (although you wouldn't be able to see it while viewing a slide) and suck up valuable system resources on the users' computer.

12 Save your work.

Creating the "States" of the Transition

In this section, the MovieClip you just created will be nested into another MovieClip that will serve as the actual transition.

1   Create a new MovieClip and give it the instance name <u>trans_mc</u>.

2   In Edit mode for the new MovieClip, add two layers (totaling three). Name the layers <u>actions</u>, <u>labels</u>, and <u>anim</u>, from top to bottom.

3   Select all the layers at Frame 30 and choose Insert > Timeline > Frame (F5).

4   On the labels layer, select Frame 1 and use the Property inspector to label the frame <u>still</u>. Insert a keyframe at Frame 10 and label it <u>fade_in</u>. Also, add the label <u>fade_out</u> to a new keyframe at Frame 20.

Tip: Frame labels are handy for keeping track of significant points in your movie because they are easy to find and read later on, but labels also offer a way to make revisions easier. For example, if you write a script that references Frame 33 of the Timeline, and the content of Frame 33 is moved during a revision, you would have to also revise the script. However, if you use a frame label to identify the frame, you can move it anywhere on the Timeline and the script will still work properly.

---

5   On Frame 1 of the anim layer, drag trans_anim to the Stage and
    position its left edge to the right of the registration mark. Using the
    Property inspector, change the alpha value to 0 so that the clip is
    invisible. Give it an instance name of <u>trans_anim</u>.

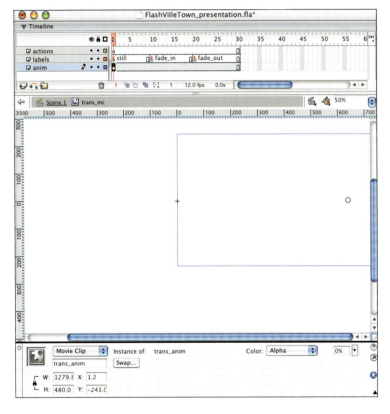

6   Still on the anim layer, insert keyframes at Frames 10, 15, 20, and 25.

7   At Frames 15 and 20, select trans_anim and set its alpha value to 100
    percent.

8   Select Frames 10 and 20 (one at a time) in the Timeline and choose
    Motion from the Tween menu in the Property inspector to initiate
    the effect of fading in and fading out.

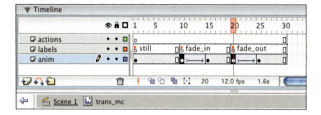

9   Save your work.

Targeting the MovieClip to Play Between Slides

The last phase of creating the transition involves targeting trans_mc with
ActionScript so that it plays between slides. When the user clicks the Back
or Forward buttons in the presentation, trans_anim (the clip inside of
trans_mc) will start playing and fade in. The main Timeline will go to the
next slide, and trans_anim will fade out and stop playing.

Note: The advantage to using templates in Flash is that some functionality is already built into them. In this case, the updateFrame()
function has been created to keep track of the current frame number.
The buttons have also been set up to run the updateFrame() function
and advance the Timeline through the presentation. Although you're
completely customizing this presentation, you can build other presentations quickly by using the templates as they are.

1   Back on the main Timeline, select Frame 1 of the actions layer and
    review the code there. You should see an updateFrame() function.

    What this does is move the playhead to the next or previous frame,
    depending on which button was clicked.

2   Locate the following code and delete it, because it will be revised:

```
forwardBtn.onPress = function() {
    updateFrame(1);
};
backBtn.onPress = function() {
    updateFrame(-1);
};
```

3   Delete the following line of code from the beginning of the script:

```
if (isLoaded == undefined) {
```

4   Delete the closing curly brace (}) of the if statement, which appears just before the line "this.isLoaded = true;" at the end of the script. Delete "this.isLoaded = true;" as well.

This removes the if statement and "unwraps" the code inside of it, allowing you to easily target the updateFrame function from within trans_mc, as you'll see in a minute.

5   Underneath the updateFrame() function, add the code in Listing 2.3 in place of the code you deleted in step 2.

Note: If you prefer to copy code from a single file instead of multiple listings, simply open **FlashVilleTown_complete.fla** and copy and paste code from it as needed.

Listing 2.3

```
forwardBtn.onPress = function() {
    trans_mc.gotoAndPlay("fade_in");
    _global.next_frame = "forward";
};
backBtn.onPress = function() {
    trans_mc.gotoAndPlay("fade_in");
    _global.next_frame = "back";
};
```

This script will tell trans_mc to play when a button is clicked and creates a variable called next_frame, which will be referenced later.

The final, revised code for Frame 1 should look like this.

```
// Define functions, handlers
// Routine to move playhead to a new frame
var updateFrame = function (inc) {
    var newFrame = _currentframe+inc;
    gotoAndStop(newFrame);
    if (_root._currentframe == 1) {
        backBtn._alpha = 50;
        backBtn.enabled = false;
    } else {
        backBtn._alpha = 100;
        backBtn.enabled = true;
    }
    if (_root._currentframe == _root._totalframes) {
        forwardBtn._alpha = 50;
        forwardBtn.enabled = false;
    } else {
        forwardBtn._alpha = 100;
        forwardBtn.enabled = true;
    }
};
// When the forward button is pressed
forwardBtn.onPress = function() {
    trans_mc.gotoAndPlay("fade_in");
    _global.next_frame = "forward";
};
backBtn.onPress = function() {
    trans_mc.gotoAndPlay("fade_in");
    _global.next_frame = "back";
};
// When the keyboard keys are pressed
var keyListener = new Object();
keyListener.onKeyDown = function() {
    if (Key.isDown(37)) {
        // Left
        trans_mc.gotoAndPlay("fade_in");
        _global.next_frame = "back";
    } else if (Key.isDown(38)) {
        // Up
        trans_mc.gotoAndPlay("fade_in");
        _global.next_frame = "start";
    } else if (Key.isDown(39)) {
        // Right
        trans_mc.gotoAndPlay("fade_in");
        _global.next_frame = "forward";
    } else if (Key.isDown(40)) {
        // Down
        trans_mc.gotoAndPlay("fade_in");
        _global.next_frame = "end";
    }
};
Key.addListener(keyListener);
// Call updateFrame to get button states correct at start
updateFrame();
stop();
```

6   Modify the keyListener script to match the following figure.

The new button code triggers the transition.

The rest of the code here can be left alone.

Listing 2.4

```
var keyListener - new Object();
keyListener.onKeyDown = function() {
    if (Key.isDown(37)) {
        // Left
        trans_mc.gotoAndPlay("fade_in");
        _global.next_frame = "back";
    } else if (Key.isDown(38)) {
        // Up
        trans_mc.gotoAndPlay("fade_in");
        _global.next_frame = "start";
    } else if (Key.isDown(39)) {
        // Right
        trans_mc.gotoAndPlay("fade_in");
        _global.next_frame = "forward";
    } else if (Key.isDown(40)) {
        // Down
        trans_mc.gotoAndPlay("fade_in");
        _global.next_frame = "end";
    }
};
```

Note: Special thanks go to Waleed Anbar at Macromedia for developing this template and working with me to make the code a great resource for learning ActionScript.

7 Double-click trans_mc in the Library to edit it. On Frame 1 of the actions layer, add a stop command:

Listing 2.5

```
stop();
```

8 On Frame 10, insert a keyframe and add this code to tell trans_anim to play:

Listing 2.6

```
trans_anim.play();
```

9 On Frame 15, insert a keyframe on the actions layer and add this code:

Listing 2.7

```
stop();
if (next_frame == "forward") {
    _root.updateFrame(1);
}
if (next_frame == "back") {
    _root.updateFrame(-1);
}
if (next_frame == "start") {
    _root.gotoAndStop(1);
}
if (next_frame == "end") {
    _root.gotoAndStop(_totalframes+1);
}
gotoAndPlay("fade_out");
```

This script checks the current value of the variable `next_frame` and then tells the `updateFrame()` function to move the main Timeline one frame forward or one frame back based on the result. Then the rest of the transition is played.

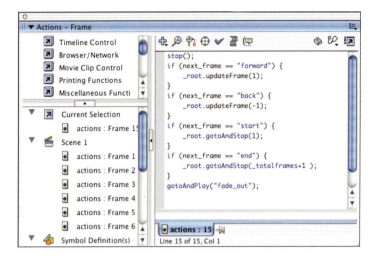

10   On Frame 25, insert a keyframe and add this code to end the transition and tell trans_anim to stop looping:

Listing 2.8

```
gotoAndStop("still");
trans_anim.gotoAndStop(1);
```

11   In Scene 1, add a new layer to the Timeline, above the buttons layer, and call it transition.

12   Drag trans_mc from the Library to the Stage (on the transition layer), align it to X = 0, Y = 0, and give it the instance name of trans_mc.

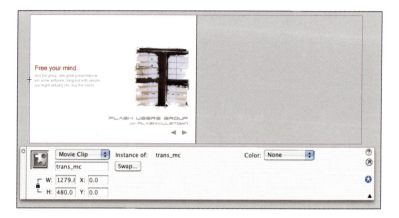

13   Choose Control > Test Movie and make sure your cool new transition is working.

14   Save your work.

Making Your Entire Presentation Printable

Next you'll make the whole presentation printable using the `PrintJob` object. The `PrintJob` object is new to ActionScript 2 and enables you to send a series of frames to the printer for simultaneous printing. You'll also write a script that will prevent the Back and Forward buttons from appearing in the printed pages.

1 On Frame 6 of the content layer on the main Timeline, drag symbol **print_btn** from the **buttons** folder in the Library to the Stage and place it between the text and the logo of slide_6. Give it the instance name print_btn.

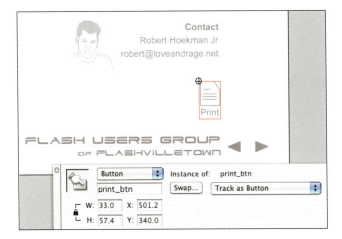

2 The slide_6_mc instance has three buttons inside of it: mmug_btn, fvt_btn, and email_btn. Add this code to Frame 6 of the actions layer to make the buttons work:

Listing 2.9

```
stop();
slide_6_mc.mmug_btn.onRelease = function() {
    getURL("http://www.macromedia.com/usergroups",
    ➥ "_blank");
};
slide_6_mc.fvt_btn.onRelease = function() {
    getURL("http://loveandrage.net", "_blank");
};
slide_6_mc.email_btn.onRelease = function() {
    getURL("mailto:robert@loveandrage.net?subject=
    ➥Inquiry from Flash Magic Reader");
};
```

This code targets the buttons inside slide_6_mc, tells them to launch a new browser window, and go to the URLs specified by the getURL commands.

3 Add this code beneath the code you just wrote:

Listing 2.10

```
function hideButtons(){
    backBtn._visible = false;
    forwardBtn._visible = false;
}
function revealButtons(){
    backBtn._visible = true;
    forwardBtn._visible = true;
}
```

When the pages of this presentation are printed, you don't want the buttons to appear, so you've added these two functions that will be called by the PrintJob script to hide and reveal them.

4 The PrintJob will be created when the print_btn is pressed. Add this code underneath the code you just added to set it up:

Listing 2.11

```
print_btn.onRelease = function(){
    hideButtons();
    my_pj = new PrintJob();
    var myResult;
    var currentFrame;
    var totalFrames = 5;
    myResult = my_pj.start();
    for(currentFrame=1;currentFrame<=totalFrames;
    ➥currentFrame++){
myResult=my_pj.addPage(0,{xMin:0,xMax:1000,yMin:0,yMax:1000},
➥null,currentFrame);
}
    my_pj.send();
    delete my_pj;
    revealButtons();
}
```

Several things happen here. First, the `hideButtons()` function makes the buttons invisible, so they don't appear in the printed pages. Second, a `PrintJob` instance is created and given the name `my_pj`. Next, three variables are created: `myResult`, `currentFrame`, and `totalFrames`. The `myResult` variable is used first to start the `PrintJob`, and then to add pages to it. The `for` script loops through frames on the main Timeline and adds them to the `PrintJob` until the first five frames (set by the `totalFrames` variable) have been spooled for the printer. The `totalFrames` variable is set to equal 5 because there's no reason to print the last slide. Finally, the `PrintJob` is sent to the printer and deleted; then the `revealButtons()` function is called to make the buttons visible again.

The following figure shows the actions for Frame 6 of the actions layer.

```
1  stop();
2  slide_6_mc.mmug_btn.onRelease = function() {
3      getURL("http://www.macromedia.com/usergroups", "_blank");
4  };
5  slide_6_mc.fvt_btn.onRelease = function() {
6      getURL("http://www.macromedia.com", "_blank");
7  };
8  slide_6_mc.email_btn.onRelease = function() {
9      getURL("mailto:robert@loveandrage.net?subject=Inquiry from Flash Magic Reader");
10 };
11 function hideButtons(){
12     backBtn._visible = false;
13     forwardBtn._visible = false;
14 }
15 function revealButtons(){
16     backBtn._visible = true;
17     forwardBtn._visible = true;
18 }
19 print_btn.onRelease = function(){
20     hideButtons();
21     my_pj = new PrintJob();
22     var myResult;
23     var currentFrame;
24     var totalFrames = 5;
25     myResult = my_pj.start();
26     for(currentFrame=1;currentFrame<=totalFrames;currentFrame++){
27 myResult=my_pj.addPage(0,{xMin:0,xMax:1000,yMin:0,yMax:1000},null,currentFrame);
28     }
29     my_pj.send();
30     delete my_pj;
31     revealButtons();
32 }
33
```

5   Save your work, and then publish the movie (File > Publish).

6   Finally, choose File > Save As Template. In the New Template dialog box, enter <u>Presentation</u> in the Name field and <u>Flash Magic</u> in the Category field. Write a short description if you would like and click Save.

7   Close FlashVilleTown_presentation.fla, and then choose File > New. When the New Document dialog box opens, look under the Templates tab in the Flash Magic category. You'll see your new template there ready to be used any time you would like.

Now Try This

By now you've learned to create a custom template, build a transition, and take advantage of authortime sharing. You've also mastered the `PrintJob` object.

Here are some ideas on how to apply the skills you've learned or use the project you've completed in other ways:

- Use transitions in a Flash-based presentation for a more engaging user experience.

- Use a `PrintJob` object in a banner ad to print a full-color brochure on-the-fly.

- Hide any frames you don't want to print and instead show a simple animation that ends with a "Print Presentation" button.

Attracting Users with a Transparent, Flash-Driven Ad

The core team at **DallaVilla Design** includes (clockwise from left) Chris DallaVilla, Ron Thompson, Drew Horton, and Rick Williams. They are dedicated to producing innovative, exciting work and have produced successful, award-winning projects for the entertainment and fashion industries.

DallaVilla Design

One of the biggest things that we've learned in running a studio focused on interactive design is that there must always be a strategy that underlies the creative work. Sure, art for art's sake is great, but when the client wants results, we'd better deliver.

Now everyone knows that standard banners work and are noticed in a limited fashion, so it was up to us, the interactive design community, to figure out a new way to catch the eye and attention of the viewer. By developing content overlay ads, we are able to work our way into a viewer's consciousness and still keep the irritation factor to a minimum. Our clients love the results and, of course, it allows us to expand past the limits of standard, rectangular banners. It keeps things interesting.

It Works Like This

In this project, you'll seamlessly integrate a Flash advertisement with HTML. Here are the basic steps of the project:

1. Develop a transparent ad that overlays existing content for a specified duration by using Flash and DHTML code.

2. Use the windowless mode parameter to make the background "color" of the ad transparent, which allows the Flash movie (advertisement) to overlay the content.

3. Set a duration of time (defined by use of the getTimer function), to dock the content as a banner ad.

You can avoid the trap of the standard banner ad.

Instead, try a seamless, transparent ad.

Preparing to Work

To prepare for this project, you will need to do the following:

1   Copy the **Projects/03** folder from the accompanying CD to your hard drive.

2   If you would like to see the finished version of the piece so you know what you'll be building, open **dvd.htm**.

3   Open a text editor or an HTML editor such as Macromedia Dreamweaver.

Setting Up the Stage

Here, you will be setting the Stage for the project, making sure that the specs are correct and creating the layers that you will use throughout. Setting these up ahead of time will eliminate any chance of confusion later on and will allow you to focus on the main parts of the project without having to stop for the basics.

1   Create a new document with these specifications:

> 31fps
> 800×250
> bgcolor=#0099FF

2   Create three new layers (for a total of four), and label the layers from top to bottom as follows:

> labels
> actions
> main animation
> end animation

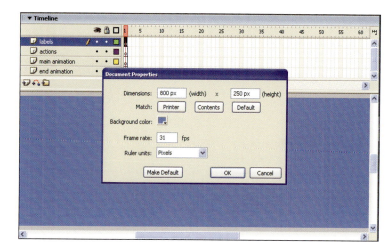

3   Save your work as example.fla.

Creating the Flash Ad

This section will lead you, step by step, through the processes involved in adding an animation to your movie (by dragging it over from a pre-existing Library) and adding the actions that will make it function.

Note: For teaching purposes, an animation called **dvd.fla** is in the **Projects/03** folder, but feel free substitute your own work.

1 On the labels layer, name the first keyframe <u>begin ad</u>.

2 On the actions layer, add this code in the actions property of the first keyframe:

Listing 3.1

```
stop();
```

Using stop on the first frame lets the main animation movie clip play.

3 Open the file **dvd.fla** from the **Projects/03** folder you copied to your hard drive during "Preparing to Work." From the Library of dvd.fla, drag and drop the **main animation** movie clip on the Stage of your example.fla file, placing the file on the main animation layer and setting its coordinates to X:–85, Y:128.

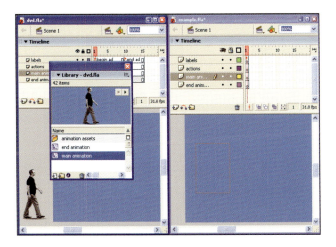

The main animation will be the actual ad—the attention-getting piece. It will be a combination of motion or sound and interactivity put together with the goal of attracting attention to the final advertisement.

Note: If your ad includes sound, you should also add a "mute" option.

Under normal circumstances, this is where you would insert the main "creativity" of your ad, which would consist of a branded, strategic representation of the selling message developed by you or your team.

In this section, you can begin interacting with your audience, so make sure that your message is clear and your functionality is well defined.

Note: Keep in mind that these are advertisements, not content. Obstructing the content that the viewer wants to gain access to can have negative consequences for the viewer, as well as ramifications from the administrators of the site of origination.

4 On the actions layer, insert a new keyframe at Frame 9. Add this code into its actions:

Listing 3.2

```
stop();
timeUp = function()
{
    _root.gotoAndStop("end ad");
    clearInterval(adTimer);
}
adTimer = setInterval(timeUp, 10000);
```

The purpose of this code snippet is to end the ad after 10 seconds by using the setInterval() function if the user has not already closed or interacted with it.

On Line 2, you assign the variable timeUp to a function. This function clears the setInterval() iteration and tells the root Timeline to gotoAndPlay("end ad"), thereby ending the advertisement.

On Line 7 you set the variable `adTimer` to the interval identifier returned by the `setInterval` function. The first argument passed to `setInterval` is a reference to the variable `timeUp`, which runs the function that ends the ad. The second argument passed is the number 10000, which is the number of milliseconds you want to pass before the ad ends itself.

Strategically, this is important because the animation exists over someone else's content, and limited duration will likely be stipulated in the advertising sales contract.

Note: According to the Internet Advertising Bureau (`www.iab.net`), any advertisement that exists as a content overlay (over page ads and pop-ups) must have an option to close. This should appear early in the animation and allow the user to "click down" the ad if he does not want to view it.

---

5   Insert a new, empty keyframe at Frame 10 for every layer on the main Timeline. On the labels layer, label this new keyframe <u>end ad</u>.

6   On the new keyframe of the actions layer, insert this code:

Listing 3.3

```
stop();
```

Stopping on the "end ad" keyframe, allowing the end animation to play and the ad to dock.

7   In the file dvd.fla, drag and drop the movie clip named **end animation** onto the Stage of example.fla, placing the movie clip on the end animation layer at the empty keyframe on Frame 10.

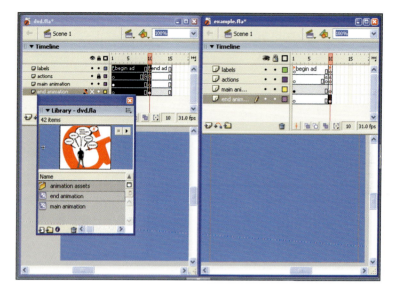

8   Highlight the movie clip and make sure that it is at these coordinates: X:501, Y:1.

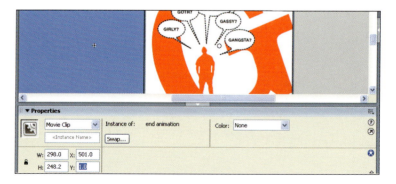

9   Export your movie, saving it with the name <u>example.swf</u>.

Integrating the Flash Ad with HTML

Finally, this section will detail how to integrate the Flash piece with the page's HTML code to function properly as an over page ad using the windowless mode parameter.

1 From the Projects/03 folder, open **flashad.htm** with a text editor or an HTML editor such as Macromedia's Dreamweaver.

2 Directly after the <body> tag, insert this DHTML code:

Listing 3.4

```
<div id="flashad" style="position:absolute; left:0;
➡top:120; width:10; height:0; z-index:1;">
```

This DHTML code defines the position of the layer that the Flash movie sits in. By setting this, you will eliminate the possibility of the ad getting lost if the viewer resizes the window.

Depending on the layout of the content page (centered versus left justified, and so on), you might need to change your layer positioning to "relative" as opposed to "absolute."

3 Insert your Flash movie into the layer:

Listing 3.5

```
<object classid="clsid:D27CDB6E-AE6D-11cf-96B8-
➡444553540000"codebase="http://download.macromedia.com/pub/
➡shockwave/cabs/flash/swflash.cab#version=6,0,29,0"
➡width="800" height="250">
    <param name="movie" value="example.swf">
    <param name="quality" value="high">
    <param name="wmode" value="transparent">
    <embed src="example.swf" width="800" height="250"
    ➡quality="high" pluginspage="http://www.macromedia.
    ➡com/go/getflashplayer" type="application/x-shockwave-
    ➡flash"wmode="transparent"></embed>
</object>
```

Pay particular attention to the param attribute named wmode. Setting this attribute to transparent indicates to the Flash Player that the background color of the Flash movie is to be transparent.

This step creates the transparency that gives the illusion that your ad exists on top of—or even as part of—the page's content. Strategically, this allows users to see the ad as more than just a pop-up that they must close down before getting to the "real" content. It creates a scenario wherein viewers are more likely to see the advertisement as interesting content, thereby paying closer attention to it and increasing the rate of retention and likelihood of action.

Note: The following browsers currently support windowless mode:

- Internet Explorer 3 or higher (Windows)
- Internet Explorer 5.1* and 5.2* (Macintosh)
- Netscape 7.0*
- Mozilla 1.0 or higher*
- AOL*
- CompuServe*

Macromedia Flash Player version 6.0.65.0 (Windows) or 6.0.67.0 (Macintosh) or higher required for this feature.

4 Close the DHTML layer by adding the following code.

Listing 3.6

```
</div>
```

5   Save your work and open example.htm in a browser. To see the finished version of the piece, refer to **dvd.swf** in the Projects/03 folder.

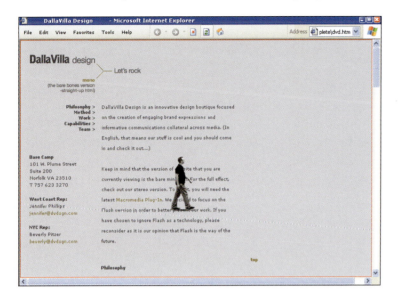

Working with Third-Party Hosts

In this project, you learned how to go about setting up an ad in an internally hosted environment. Realistically, however, you will likely find yourself creating ads that will be hosted by one of several third-party ad hosts, such as the following:

• Eyeblaster (www.eyeblaster.com)

• Unicast (www.unicast.com)

• Point Roll (www.pointroll.com)

• Doubleclick (www.doubleclick.com)

• MaxWorldwide (www.maxworldwide.com)

• focusIN Specialty Web Network (www.focusin.com)

• 24/7 Media (www.247realmedia.com)

In addition to handling the serving of the ad, many of these hosts offer tracking services. Upon reaching an agreement, these hosts will give you code snippets to add to your Flash files that will track a number of different information types. This can provide valuable marketing information and can aid in assessing return on investment for your clients.

Another attractive offering of these third-party hosts is an easy-to-use interface for designers to upload prospective ads and see how they will work in a real environment. These interfaces allow the host to check for variables that are of extreme importance when running any banner campaign, but content overlay ads, in particular. Uploading your ads through one of these will ensure that the file size, Flash Player version and code are correct. When the time is right, they will also allow you to present the ad to your client as it will appear when fully functional.

Finally, these hosts will also be able to offer insight into the specific requirements of individual outlets. While it would be nice for every outlet to adhere to the same standards and guidelines, such is rarely the case. The teams at each of these hosts will be able to provide information that will save you time and effort and, most importantly, keep your ad from being rejected.

Now Try This

In this project, you've developed an ad that overlays existing content by integrating Flash and DHTML. You've also used the windowless mode parameter and the getTimer function to display and dock the ad. You can add a number of features to this framework to make more engaging online advertisements.

Here are some ideas on how to apply the skills you've learned or use the project you've completed in other ways:

- Add video and audio elements, or user-driven selection fields. By experimenting with these elements, you can create ads with a number of different levels of interactivity to suit the varying interest levels of your audience. You can even help further drive up the interest quotient.

- Try working with other banner formats. In addition to making an ad that "floats" over content, there are any number of expandable banner options that will allow you to use these techniques and will allow you to develop an eye-catching ad that has a lower CPM. Your clients will love you for it. Banners that expand or contract over content can make an otherwise boring banner campaign something to talk about.

- Try to adhere to Internet Advertising Bureau guidelines for pixels and downloads. Initial downloads should be minimal to have your ad begin as soon as the page launches. After the initial ad is loaded and a user clicks on your ad, further downloads are acceptable.

- Also, when developing an ad for a specific outlet, such as Yahoo or AOL, remember to check with them to make sure that they do not have site-specific requirements and restrictions. Most outlets that support these ads will have a page dedicated to advertising specs and a contact who can answer specific questions. Use these!

- The designs for ads of this nature inherently depend on the content over which they will play. Consider the backgrounds (text, colors, and so on) that the underlying page provides rather than risk creating an ad that gets lost among the content or is rejected by an outlet. For ads that are being created for use on multiple pages, consider using solid backgrounds to minimize these risks.

- Add a clickTAG, which is the tracking code that the ad-serving network assigns to an individual ad. clickTAG allows the network to register where the ad was displayed, when it was clicked on, and also defines where (a specific URL) the user will go when he takes action. This click-through data is reported to the ad-serving hosts so that advertisers can determine the effectiveness of their campaign.

Creating Electronic Haiku with a Sound Mixing Toy

Aria Danika
is an interactive
developer/artist, senior
moderator at Flashkit.com,
and member of the
Hypermedia Research
Centre in London.

Aria Danika
with Geisha artwork by Chris Norman

My early experiments and fascination with sound toys and generative music—the idea of creating sound output through interactive design interfaces—goes back to my days as a graduate student at the Hypermedia Research Centre in London. This fascination continues to the current day, and has so far led to a series of sound toys developed in Flash and Director.

The genre of sound toys has evolved thanks to experimentation by interactive designers and video game developers who seek to create interactive music experiences. They accomplish this by designing simple interfaces that allow the user to manipulate sounds, explore rhythm, and engage in a playful exploration of music composition. In the book *Noise: A Political Economy of Music* (University of Minnesota Pr., 1985), author Jacques Attali predicted a break in the cultural consumption of music from the recorded item (repetition), to a situation where consumption is creation (composition). As technology advances, interactive music will undoubtedly develop beyond "frozen" performances into new forms, aesthetics, and multi-user experiences.

It Works Like This

In this project, the interface is a grid that is made of boxes (objects) that are stored in the Library and manipulated through code. The user will be able to preview sounds, play and loop selected tracks, and adjust the volume during playtime.

The root of your movie will have two main sections. The first portion contains a chunk of code that runs as soon as the movie is loaded, initializes all the properties of your instrument, and draws the visuals on the Stage. The second portion checks for user interaction, plays back sounds, and controls the playhead and volume slider. Here are the basic steps of the project:

1 Use ActionScript to generate the base grid.

2 Generate the mixer interface dynamically and align it to the center of the Stage.

3 Attach the sounds to the interface dynamically from the Library by referencing them with a Linkage ID.

4 Use movie clip events (onPress()), methods (createEmptyMovieClip()), and Sound Object methods (start()) to build the interactivity and interface controls, such as playhead and the Sound Volume slider.

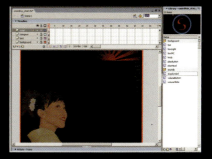
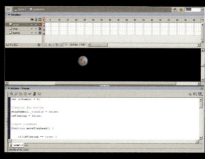

For this sound mixing toy, create the interface and add interactivity.

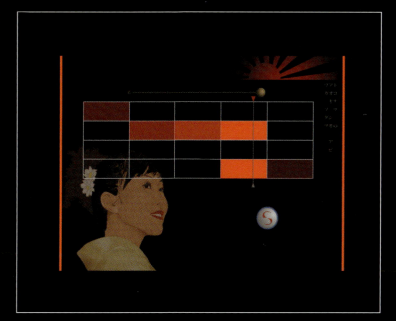

The result is a self-created, ever-changing sountrack.

Preparing to Work

To prepare for this project, you will need to do the following:

1 Copy the **Projects/04** folder to your hard drive.

2 Open **soundtoy_final.swf** to see how the project works. Close it when you're finished.

> **Note:** Some of the best mixing toys are ambient beautiful abstractions with an interface that is simple enough to be used without instructions, that encourages participation rather than technique, and that does not draw visual metaphors from what the user is already familiar with (such as mixing desks, jukeboxes, and turntables).

Building the Base Grid

Before you get started with adding and manipulating sounds, you need to build the various interface elements that will enable the user to interact with this game, starting with the grid: a number of boxes (or cells) grouped together that will store the sounds you have in the Library.

> **Note:** To make the project as flexible as possible, you will want to make everything but the static images build themselves dynamically. This allows you to add more sounds, or change the look of your instrument, and have it apply to the entire movie easily.

1 Start by declaring all the variables. Open **soundtoy_start.fla** from the **Projects/04** folder you copied to your hard drive during "Preparing to Work."

The Timeline of the main movie has four layers: background, text, risingsun, and script. You'll use the script layer to store your actions. The bottom three layers contain all the static background graphics of the game, such as the geisha, the rising sun, and the haiku text.

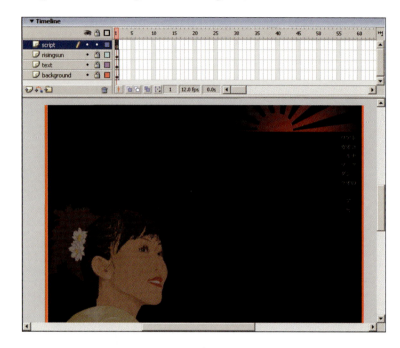

2 Click on the script layer and open the Actions panel.

3 On Frame 1, add this script to declare the variables. Note that you are scripting using the Actions panel in what used to be known as Expert mode in previous versions of Flash.

Listing 4.1

```
onLoad = function(){

    //constants
    _global.ROWS            = 4;
    _global.COLUMNS         = 5;
    _global.BOXWIDTH        = 100;
    _global.BOXHEIGHT       = 40;
    _global.DEFAULTBOXALPHA = 30;
    _global.SPEED           = 5;

    //variables
    var x,y            :Number = 0;
    var soundNum       :Number = 0;
}
```

The following figure shows what your code looks like at this point.

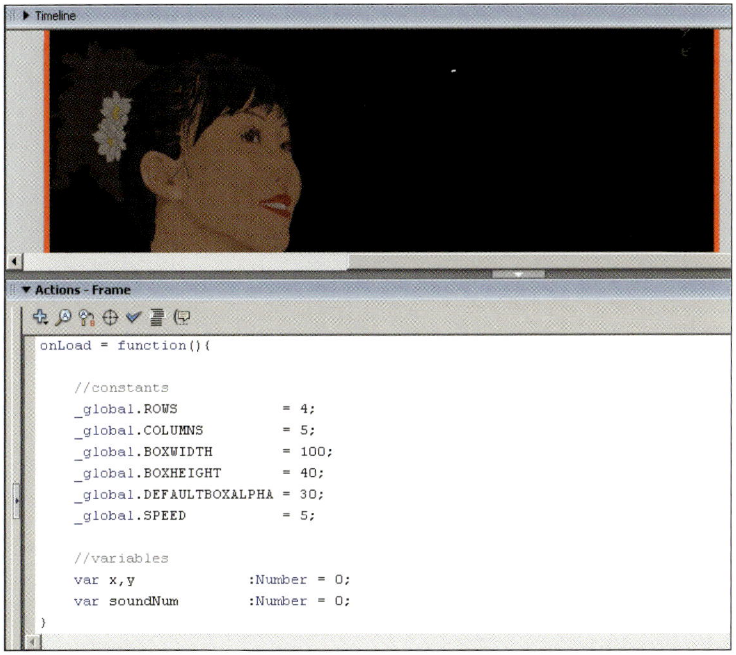

Here, you have written an initialization function so that you can build your project dynamically.

By associating this with the onLoad movie clip method, you can make sure that the construction happens on the first frame of the .swf file and is transparent to the user.

Following that, you insert the variables that will define the parameters of the grid, such as width, height, alpha value, and playback motion. Note that these values are constant and should not be changed.

```
    _global.ROWS            = 4;
    _global.COLUMNS         = 5;
    _global.BOXWIDTH        = 100;
    _global.BOXHEIGHT       = 40;
    _global.DEFAULTBOXALPHA = 30;
    _global.SPEED           = 5;
```

Defining these variables as global will make them accessible to every timeline in your movie, and prevent you from having to refer to _root or _parent.

```
    var x,y            :Number = 0;
    var soundNum       :Number = 0;
```

These variables are defined as being of the type Number, which will prevent them from being filled with a different type of value (doing so will return an error).

4 Save your work.

Note: You can also check the syntax of your script at this stage, as shown in the following figure, to ensure there aren't any errors. Just click on the Check Syntax box in the Actions panel. It's good practice to test your movie and check your code during the development process.

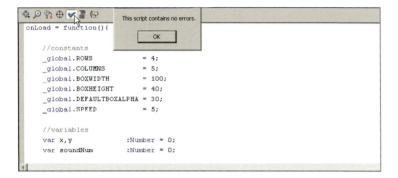

Generating the Mixer Interface

Having defined the parameters of the grid (width, height, and number of columns and rows), you can now build it by using ActionScript. For this, you need to attach instances of the boxMC movie clip from the Library, position them, and align them on the Stage. To do this, you need to assign a Linkage ID to the boxMC movie clip so that you can refer to it through ActionScript.

1   Open the movie Library (Ctrl/Cmd+L).

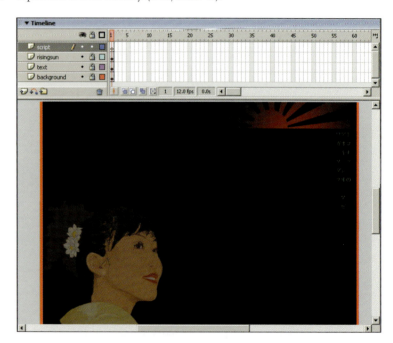

2   Select the boxMC movie clip. Right-click/Ctrl-click and select the Linkage option.

3   In the Linkage Properties panel, select Export for ActionScript. The identifier name, boxMC, is inserted automatically.

Click the OK button to close the Linkage Properties window.

4   Click on the first frame of the script layer and insert the following script right after the soundNum variable and before the }:

Listing 4.2

```
//Grid development
  createEmptyMovieClip("movieGrid", 1);

//Set initial volume
  movieGrid.soundVolume = 100;
  movieGrid.gridColumnCount = 0;

//Attaching the individual cells of the grid.
//Setting height and width.
  for(x=0;x<ROWS;x++) {
    for(y=0;y<COLUMNS;y++) {
      var boxName:String = "boxMC"+x+"_"+y;
      movieGrid.attachMovie("boxMC",boxName,10*x+y);
      movieGrid[boxName]._width = BOXWIDTH;
      movieGrid[boxName]._height = BOXHEIGHT;
      movieGrid[boxName]._x = movieGrid[boxName].
      ➡ _width * y;
      movieGrid[boxName]._y = movieGrid[boxName].
      ➡ _height * x;
      movieGrid[boxName].boxLight._alpha = DEFAULTBOXALPHA;
    }
  }
```

The following figure shows what your code should look like at this point.

```
//Grid development
createEmptyMovieClip("movieGrid", 1);

//Set initial volume
movieGrid.soundVolume = 100;
movieGrid.gridColumnCount = 0;

//Attaching the individual cells of the grid.
//Setting height and width.
for(x=0;x<ROWS;x++) {
    for(y=0;y<COLUMNS;y++) {
        var boxName:String = "boxMC"+x+"_"+y;
        movieGrid.attachMovie("boxMC",boxName,10*x+y);
        movieGrid[boxName]._width = BOXWIDTH;
        movieGrid[boxName]._height = BOXHEIGHT;
        movieGrid[boxName]._x = movieGrid[boxName]._width * y;
        movieGrid[boxName]._y = movieGrid[boxName]._height * x;
        movieGrid[boxName].boxLight._alpha = DEFAULTBOXALPHA;
    }
}
}
```

Here you have created a container movie clip, named movieGrid, so that you can have more control as to where your dynamically generated grid appears on the Stage. We set the initial volume soundVolume to 100 and the gridColumnCount to 0.

A nested loop will build your grid dynamically, working much like a typewriter. It will add a new box to the right of the previous one until it creates the number defined by the COLUMNS variable, and then it will move on to the next row and continue until the entire grid is built.

5   Test your movie by choosing Ctrl+Enter/Cmd+Return.

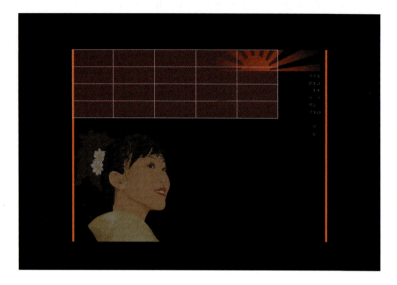

The grid is aligned at the top-left corner of the movie, which isn't ideal, and it's not doing anything just yet. You will work on positioning it in the center, but not before you add the sounds.

6   Save your work.

Adding Sounds

Now that the grid is generated, you can attach the sounds (all 20 of them) from the Library to each box. Before you start writing the code, you need to reference each sound by assigning a Linkage ID to it.

1   Open the **sounds** folder in the Library.

2   Select the first one, **ARIA_S1_MP3**.

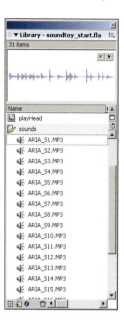

3   Right-click/Ctrl-click and select the Linkage option.

4   In the Linkage Properties panel, select Export for ActionScript.

5   Type in the identifier for the Linkage ID: <u>sound0</u>.

6   Repeat Steps 3–5 for the remaining 19 sounds in the Library, where **ARIA_S2.MP3** has linkage ID <u>sound1</u>, **ARIA_S3.MP3** has <u>sound2</u>, and so on.

7   Select the script layer (main movie). Click on Frame 1.

8   Enter this code right after your `movieGrid` development code and before the last `}`:

Listing 4.3

```
//Attaching sounds
    movieGrid[boxName].sound = new Sound();
    movieGrid[boxName].soundNum = soundNum;
    movieGrid[boxName].sound.attachSound("sound"+soundNum);
    soundNum++;
```

Your actions for this frame should now look like this:

```
onLoad = function(){

  //constants
  _global.ROWS            = 4;
  _global.COLUMNS         = 5;
  _global.BOXWIDTH        = 100;
  _global.BOXHEIGHT       = 40;
  _global.DEFAULTBOXALPHA = 30;
  _global.SPEED           = 5;
  //variables
  var x,y                 :Number = 0;
  var soundNum            :Number = 0;

  //Grid development
  createEmptyMovieClip("movieGrid", 1);

  //Set initial volume
  movieGrid.soundVolume = 100;
  movieGrid.gridColumnCount = 0;

  //Attaching the individual cells of the grid.
  //Setting height and width.
  for(x=0;x<ROWS;x++) {
  for(y=0;y<COLUMNS;y++) {
  var boxName:String = "boxMC"+x+"_"+y;
  movieGrid.attachMovie("boxMC",boxName,10*x+y);
  movieGrid[boxName]._width = BOXWIDTH;
  movieGrid[boxName]._height = BOXHEIGHT;
  movieGrid[boxName]._x = movieGrid[boxName]._width * y;
  movieGrid[boxName]._y = movieGrid[boxName]._height * x;
  movieGrid[boxName].boxLight._alpha = DEFAULTBOXALPHA;
```

```
  //Attaching sounds
    movieGrid[boxName].sound = new Sound();
    movieGrid[boxName].soundNum = soundNum;
    movieGrid[boxName].sound.attachSound("sound"+soundNum);
    soundNum++;
  }
 }
}
```

Each time through the loop, an instance of the boxMC movie clip (located in the movie's Library) will be placed on the Stage and given an instance name and level based on its row and column. After this instance is on the Stage, you can create a new sound object, and by using the `attachSound()` method, you can attach one of the Library's sounds to it. (These will be named **sound0–sound19** in this movie.)

By using sound objects, you don't have to drag the sound from the Library onto the Stage, and you can use the methods and properties of the sound object to manipulate your sounds.

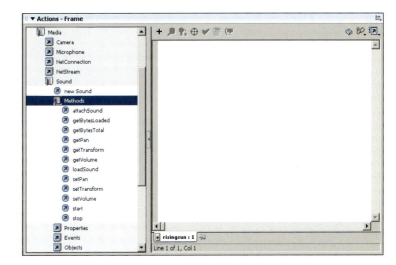

Finally, you add one to the `soundNum` variable, so the next sound attached is the next in the sequence. The sounds, when attached, will follow this pattern:

    0 1 2 3 4
    5 6 7 8 9
    10 11 12 13 14
    15 16 17 18 19

9   Save your work.

Scripting the Music Boxes

You can now focus on adding some interface elements that will enable the user to interact with this sound toy and mix the sounds. For this project, you will build a playhead, a PLAY/STOP button, and a Volume Control slider. Before you start scripting each one of those elements, however, you need to add some actions to the boxMC movie clip that will enable the user to preview the sounds and adjust the transparency (_alpha) of each box in the grid accordingly.

1   Double-click on the boxMC movie clip in the Library to go into Edit mode. The boxMC has been assigned the instance name boxLight.

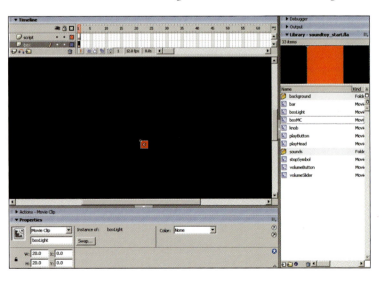

2   Go to the script layer and click on Frame 1.

3   Insert this script:

Listing 4.4

```
var activated:Boolean = false;
boxLight._alpha = 0;
```

This script sets the variable `activated` to `false`. and the `_alpha` property of the boxLight movie clip to 0 (full transparency). The variable `activated` is defined as a Boolean type.

4   Add the following code after the last statement of the previous script:

Listing 4.5

```
onRelease = function () {
    if(activated==false){
        activated = true;
        boxLight._alpha = DEFAULTBOXALPHA;
        if(_parent.playButton.isPlaying == false) {
            sound.start();
        }
    } else {
        sound.stop("sound"+soundNum);
        activated = false;
        boxLight._alpha = 0;
    }
}
```

The `onRelease()` function controls the boxMC movie clip both when it's activated (user clicks on it) and when it's not (`activated = false`).

When the user clicks on a box, then the _alpha of the **boxLight** movie clip is set to `DEFAULTBOXALPHA` (which has a value of 30) and the sound starts playing.

If `activated` is `true`, then `sound.stop("sound"+soundNum);` allows the user to click on a box anytime during the preview and stop the sound associated with it.

In Step 5 you finalize the code for the boxMC by scripting the last part, which is the _alpha fade.

5   After the following three lines

```
boxLight._alpha = 0;
    }
}
```

type this code:

Listing 4.6

```
onEnterFrame = function() {
    if(activated == true && boxLight._alpha >
    ➥DEFAULTBOXALPHA) {
        boxLight._alpha--;
    }
}
```

The `onEnterFrame()` function fades the `alpha` value of the boxes if two conditions are met:

```
activated == true  AND  boxLight._alpha > DEFAULTBOXALPHA
```

6   Save your work.

Scripting the Playhead

Just as you generated the grid dynamically earlier in this chapter (see the "Generating the Mixer Interface" section), you will also use ActionScript to attach the playhead dynamically so that it is always positioned relative to the size of your variable-defined grid.

You'll begin with the **playHead** movie clip, which consists of an upper arrow (graphic), a center bar (**bar** movie clip), and a bottom arrow (**knob** movie clip). The challenge comes with sizing the bar to match the grid. You will accomplish this by scaling the bar to the height of your `movieGrid` container and placing the bottom arrow below that.

1   Double-click on the **playHead** movie clip in the Library and enter Edit mode.

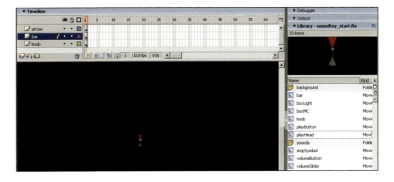

2   Click on the **knob** movie clip on the Stage. Using the Properties panel, assign to it the instance name <u>knob</u>.

3   Click on the **bar** movie clip on the Stage. Assign to it the instance name <u>bar</u>.

4   Right-click/Ctrl-click on the **playHead** movie clip in the Library and select Linkage.

5   Select the Export for ActionScript option. The identifier name playHead is inserted automatically.

6   Go back to the main Timeline. Select Frame 1 of the script layer.

7   After the following three lines

```
soundNum++;
    }
  }
```

add this script:

Listing 4.7

```
//Building the Playhead and placing it on the Stage
movieGrid.attachMovie("playHead","playHead",10000);
movieGrid.playHead.bar._height = movieGrid._height;
movieGrid.playHead.knob._y = movieGrid._height;
movieGrid.playHead._x -= BOXWIDTH/COLUMNS;
```

This script checks the height of the **movieGrid** movie clip and, based on that value, it stretches the **bar** movie clip and positions the knob at the bottom of the **movieGrid**.

8   Save your work.

Scripting the PLAY/STOP Button

For the playHead to be triggered, however, you need user input. Here's where the PLAY/STOP button comes in. You'll use one object for the button and script it so that the button can have multiple functionality. This button will need to do the following:

- Stop all active sound previews, and then play back the sequence.
- Allow the playhead to move.
- Stop all the sounds.
- Reset the playhead to its starting position.

Note: Rather than creating two buttons to stop and play, you use a two-frame movie clip called playButton. This allows you to dynamically attach and position the movie clip on the Stage from the Library by using the `attachMovie()` method.

---

1   Select the **playButton** movie clip in the Library. Right-click and select Linkage.

2   In the Linkage Properties panel, select the Export for ActionScript option.

The movie clip's name, playButton, is automatically inserted as the linkage identifier.

3   Double-click the playButton movie clip to enter Edit mode for this movie clip.

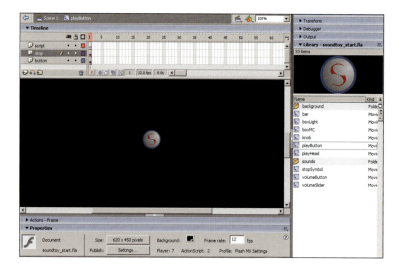

The Timeline of this movie clip has three layers named: button, stop, and script. The stop layer has the stopSymbol movie clip, which sits on top of the button. When the stopSymbol is showing (`visibility = true`), then the button becomes a Stop button. When it's not showing (`visibility = false`), then the button becomes a Play button.

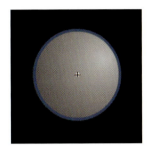

4   Go to Frame 1 of the script layer and add the code in Listing 4.9. The script layer is where you'll store your actions.

Listing 4.8

```
var z:Number = 0;

//script for button
stopSymbol._visible = false;
isPlaying = false;
```

Here, you set the variable z to 0—this variable is scoped to this movie clip. You then set variable `isPlaying` to <u>false</u>, telling the movie whether or not the Play button has been pressed and set the visibility of the `stopSymbol` to <u>false</u>.

5   Enter the following code right after the last statement of the previous script:

Listing 4.9

```
//move playHead
function movePlayhead() {

    if(isPlaying == true) {
        if(_parent.playHead._x < BOXWIDTH*COLUMNS) {
            _parent.playHead._x += SPEED;
        } else {
            _parent.playHead._x = 0;
            _parent.gridColumnCount = 0;
        }
    }
}
```

The `movePlayhead()` function controls the movement of the playhead across the X axis.

The first condition looks at when `isPlaying == true`. If it is `true`, then we can start moving the playhead to the right, in increments determined by our speed variable. If it is `false`, then we will jump back to the waiting position, to the left of `movieGrid`.

The `playHead` will move for as long as its `_x` value is less than `BOXWIDTH*COLUMNS` (the rightmost edge of the grid). Otherwise (`else`) the playhead will be reset (`playHead_x = 0`).

6   Add this code to the `movePlayhead()` function:

Listing 4.10

```
//check position, play sound(s) and light the cell(s)
if(Math.floor(_parent.playHead._x/BOXWIDTH) ==
➡ _parent.gridColumnCount) {
   if(_parent.gridColumnCount < COLUMNS) {
      trace(_parent.gridColumnCount);
         for(z=0;z<ROWS;z++) {
        var boxName:String =
         ➡"boxMC"+z+"_"+_parent.gridColumnCount;
         if(_parent[boxName].activated == true) {
parent[boxName].sound.setVolume(_parent.soundVolume);
parent[boxName].sound.start();
parent[boxName].boxLight._alpha = 100;
         }
      }
   }

//add one to gridColumnCount
   _parent.gridColumnCount++;
      }
   }
}
```

This code assigned the `"boxMC"+z+"_"+_parent.gridColumnCount` to a variable named `boxName`, which makes calling it much easier and prevents the Flash player from having to calculate this value repeatedly. Here the script checks for the position of the playhead and if `parent[boxName].activated == true`, then it starts the sound, sets its volume to the value of `_parent.soundVolume` (which was defined in the main timeline), and sets the `_alpha` property of the boxLight to 100.

7   Add the following script:

Listing 4.11

```
onRelease = function() {
   stopAllSounds();

   if (isPlaying==false) {
      movieGrid.playHead._x=0;
      isPlaying = true;
      stopSymbol._visible = true;
      playSounds = setInterval (movePlayhead, 60);
   } else {
      isPlaying = false;
      stopSymbol._visible = false;
      clearInterval(playSounds);
      _parent.playHead._x = 0-BOXWIDTH/COLUMNS;
      _parent.gridColumnCount = 0;
   }

}
```

When the button is pressed, the command will be given to stop all sounds because sound playback will now be dependent on the `playHead`.

If the `playHead` is not currently in motion (`isPlaying==false`), pressing the button will make the playhead jump to the start of the grid, indicate that it is active, and start the motion. Setting the `_visible` property of `stopSymbol` will indicate to the user that pressing the button a second time will stop the playback.

To make the Timeline move independently of the movie's frame rate, the `setInterval` function is used, and calls the `movePlayhead()` function that was just created every 60 milliseconds (or 60 times per second). Increasing this value will make the playhead move slower. This `setInterval()` call is being assigned to a variable (`playSounds`) so that it can be stopped when the user presses the stop button. Otherwise, it would run indefinitely.

Now, if the user presses the button again, the stopSymbol will turn invisible, the playHead will jump back to its resting position, and the playButton functionality will revert to a play button. gridColumnCount will also be reinitialized to 0, because the playHead is no longer moving.

The next and final step is to position the playButton on Stage and align it.

8   Go to the main Timeline (Scene 1). Click on Frame 1 of the script layer.

9   Add the following script right after the movieGrid.playHead._x -= BOXWIDTH/COLUMNS; statement:

Listing 4.12

```
//Building and positioning the Button
movieGrid.attachMovie("playButton","playButton",20000);
movieGrid.playButton._x = movieGrid._width -
(BOXWIDTH+movieGrid.playButton._width/2);
movieGrid.playButton._y = movieGrid._height + BOXHEIGHT;
```

Here you position the playButton dynamically on Stage by attaching an instance of the playButton movie clip to the movieGrid movie clip and setting its x and y properties relative to the size of the movieGrid. That is:

```
playButton._x = movieGrid._width -
(BOXWIDTH+movieGrid.playButton._width/2)
```

and

```
 playButton._y = movieGrid._height + BOXHEIGHT
```

10   Save your work.

Adding the Volume Control Slider

The Volume Control slider is the last element of this interface that gives more control to the user through the Sound Object and its properties. You will also use ActionScript to place this movie clip dynamically on the Stage, but before that, you need to construct it.

1   Right-click/Ctrl-click the **volumeSlider** movie clip in the Library. Select Linkage.

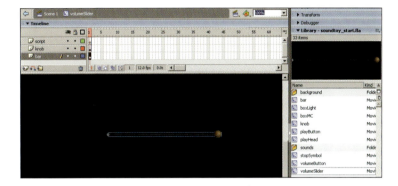

2   In the Linkage Properties panel, select Export for ActionScript. The identifier for the Linkage ID volumeSlider is automatically inserted.

3   Go to the script layer. Click Frame 1.

4   In the Actions panel, insert this script:

Listing 4.13

```
var btnLoc:Number = 0;

//when knob is pressed, allowing dragging along the x axis
volume_btn.onPress = function() {
volume_btn.startDrag(true,0,0,300,0);
}

//when knob is released, stop dragging and set the sound
➡volume
volume_btn.onRelease = volume_btn.onReleaseOutside =
➡function() {
    volume_btn.stopDrag();
    btnLoc = Math.floor(volume_btn._x/3);
    _parent.soundVolume = btnLoc;
    for(x=0;x<ROWS;x++) {
        for(y=0;y<COLUMNS;y++) {
            _parent["boxMC"+x+"_"+y].sound.setVolume(btnLoc);
        }
    }
}
```

First, you define a variable named btnLoc (type Number). This local variable will be used to store the position of the volume_btn on the volumeSlider bar.

volume_btn.onPress is a Button method that will activate when the user presses the wooden-looking ball on the slider. startDrag is a button method that is being passed five parameters: true tells the function that the dragging will be constrained (rather than letting the user drag the button anywhere on the stage), and the next four values define the constraints (left, right, top, and bottom). left and right here are the edges of the slider bar.

onRelease and onReleaseOutside are two more Button methods which are nested, because they should have the same functionality and trigger when the button is released.

stopDrag() will stop the button from moving, and the variable btnLoc will be assigned the current location of the button on the bar, divided by 3 (the bar is 300 pixels wide, and you want a volume value between 0 and 100).

soundVolume will be set to this newly created value, and then a loop will set the volume of every box in the grid using the Sound setVolume method.

5   Go back to the main movie (Scene 1). Click on Frame 1 (script layer), and insert this script to position the Volume slider on the Stage:

Listing 4.14

```
//Building and Positioning the volume slider
movieGrid.attachMovie("volumeSlider","volumeSlider",30000);
movieGrid.volumeSlider._x = BOXWIDTH -
➡(BOXWIDTH/COLUMNS)/COLUMNS;
movieGrid.volumeSlider._y -= BOXHEIGHT/2;
```

Here you are attaching an instance of the volumeSlider movie clip to the movieGrid movie clip and aligning it to the top center of the movieGrid instance.

6   Save your work.

Putting It All Together

With all the elements in place and contained within the `movieGrid` instance, you can position the whole unit centrally in your movie.

1   Click Frame 1 (the script layer) in the main movie.

2   Insert the following script after the volume slider positioning script:

Listing 4.15

```
//Positioning all attached elements
movieGrid._x = ((Stage.width/2) -
(movieGrid._width/2))+(BOXWIDTH/COLUMNS)/COLUMNS;
movieGrid._y = ((Stage.height/2) -
➥(movieGrid._height/2))+BOXHEIGHT/2;
```

Here, you define the `_x` and `_y` properties of the `movieGrid` instance so that it is centrally positioned. These values will be flexible based on the `rows` and `columns` variables.

The following figure shows what the full script looks like at this point.

```
onLoad = function(){

    //constants
    _global.ROWS            = 4;
    _global.COLUMNS         = 5;
    _global.BOXWIDTH        = 100;
    _global.BOXHEIGHT       = 40;
    _global.DEFAULTBOXALPHA = 30;
    _global.SPEED           = 5;

    //variables
    var x,y           :Number = 0;
    var soundNum      :Number = 0;

    //Grid development
    createEmptyMovieClip("movieGrid", 1);

    //Set initial volume
    movieGrid.soundVolume = 100;
    movieGrid.gridColumnCount = 0;

    //Attaching the individual cells of the grid.
    //Setting height and width.
    for(x=0;x<ROWS;x++) {
        for(y=0;y<COLUMNS;y++) {
            var boxName:String = "boxMC"+x+"_"+y;
            movieGrid.attachMovie("boxMC",boxName,10*x+y);
            movieGrid[boxName]._width = BOXWIDTH;
            movieGrid[boxName]._height = BOXHEIGHT;
            movieGrid[boxName]._x = movieGrid[boxName]._width * y;
            movieGrid[boxName]._y = movieGrid[boxName]._height * x;
            movieGrid[boxName].boxLight._alpha = DEFAULTBOXALPHA;

            //Attaching sounds
            movieGrid[boxName].sound = new Sound();
            movieGrid[boxName].soundNum = soundNum;
            movieGrid[boxName].sound.attachSound("sound"+soundNum);
            soundNum++;
        }
    }
    //Building the Playhead and placing it on the Stage
    movieGrid.attachMovie("playHead","playHead",10000);
    movieGrid.playHead.bar._height = movieGrid._height;
    movieGrid.playHead.knob._y = movieGrid._height;
    movieGrid.playHead._x -= BOXWIDTH/COLUMNS;

    //Building and positioning the Button
    movieGrid.attachMovie("playButton","playButton",20000);
    movieGrid.playButton._x = movieGrid._width - (BOXWIDTH+movieGrid.playButton._width/2);
    movieGrid.playButton._y = movieGrid._height + BOXHEIGHT;

    //Building and Positioning the volume slider
    movieGrid.attachMovie("volumeSlider","volumeSlider",30000);
    movieGrid.volumeSlider._x = BOXWIDTH - (BOXWIDTH/COLUMNS)/COLUMNS;
    movieGrid.volumeSlider._y -= BOXHEIGHT/2;

    //Positioning all attached elements
    movieGrid._x = ((Stage.width/2) - (movieGrid._width/2))+(BOXWIDTH/COLUMNS)/COLUMNS;
    movieGrid._y = ((Stage.height/2) - (movieGrid._height/2))+BOXHEIGHT/2;
}
```

3   Test your movie and preview some sounds; click a box and click again to deselect it. If you are happy with your selections, click the Play button and enjoy your composition.

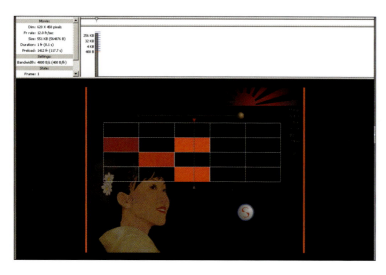

4   Save your work.

Now Try This

By now you've created a chunk of code that runs as soon as your movie is loaded, initializes all the properties of your instrument, and draws the visuals. You've also learned to check for user interaction and play back sounds.

Here are some ideas on how to apply the skills you've learned or use the project you've completed in other ways:

- As your sound toys grow more complex and you use many sound loops, you might want to consider using a preloader or optimizing and trimming your loops to keep the file size down. You can also experiment using the Sound object methods, such as getBytesTotal() and getBytesLoaded(), to preload your sounds apart from the rest of the movie.

- You could also load your sounds from an external source (using the loadSound() method of the Sound object). This allows you to edit and update your MP3 samples outside of the Flash authoring environment and will reduce your initial movie size significantly.

- Create an interface that allows for user input from more than one player. Each player can have access to a grid that plays a sequence and engages with the other players to compose a collaborative complex musical performance.

Designing and Scoring a Pac-Man Style Maze Game

Aria Danika

is an interactive developer/artist, senior moderator at Flashkit.com, and member of the Hypermedia Research Centre in London.

Aria Danika

with character design by Chris Norman

I grew up playing games. However, most of my early experiences with video games were limited to arcades, friends' houses, and trying to convince my parents that an Atari 2600 was something no family should be without.

One of my favorite early games and sources of inspiration was a simple, random-generated maze titled *Diamaze* (1990), designed by Steve Herring. Diamaze was a puzzle/maze game where you have about a minute to collect as many diamonds as you can, using your keyboard arrow keys, before the lights go out.

Tile-based games have been around for a very long time and can serve as a clever way to build a game environment without consuming too much memory. The main aspect of this technique involves slicing up your game background into reusable square blocks. Then you place them together (tile) using code in order to build a map that acts as the data structure for the game. This technique is similar to the concept of using reusable symbols in your Flash movie to save time and space.

It Works Like This

This game is constructed using *tiles* (also known as *cells)*, which are square graphics stored as movie clips. These are "tiled" using ActionScript to generate the game environment: a top-down maze. Complete with sound effects and a scoring feature, users are able to use the arrow keys to move the character and collect balloons. Here are the basic steps of the project:

1   Attach the script that allows the user to begin the game.

2   Attach two reusable tree maze tiles dynamically with ActionScript to construct the game field.

3   Insert the main character dynamically, by assigning Linkage properties to the movie clip.

4   Write a custom collision-detection script that calculates the position of the main character against the bounds of the tree tiles and the balloons.

5   Set up the character movement by creating motion Listeners that check for key presses.

6   Keep game score by counting the number of collisions with collectable items and displaying the output in a text field.

7   Attach sound effects to provide feedback to your user when he is interacting with your game.

To begin, you'll set up the character introduction and maze.

Then the fun begins. See how many balloons you can collect.

Preparing to Work

To prepare for this project, you will need to do the following:

1 Copy the **Projects/05** folder to your hard drive.

2 Open **maze_final.swf** and play through the game. Close it when you're finished.

Creating the Game Intro

Games, like life, are all about interaction. Unlike life, however, most games come with a set of instructions. This Pac-Man–style game has an introduction that serves both to introduce the character Puffin to the user and to offer a brief set of instructions for the game. Here, you will attach a script to the Enter button that will allow the user to enter the maze and begin the game.

1 Open the **maze_start.fla** file from the **Projects/05** folder you copied to your hard drive during "Preparing to Work."

   The game intro is in the first scene, Game intro.

The Scene panel (Windows > Design panels > Scene or Shift+F2) lists the two scenes of the maze game.

2 Click on the Enter button on the Stage and, using the Properties panel, give it the instance name intro_btn.

3 Open the Actions panel, go to the actions layer in Frame 1 of this layer, and add this script:

Listing 5.1

```
//Button code - jumps to scene 2
stop();
intro_btn.onRelease = function() {
    nextScene();
}
```

This script executes when the user releases the Enter button. You target the button instance intro_btn with a script on the main Timeline that instructs the player to jump to the next scene. The next scene (Tree Maze) is where the user can play the game.

n instance name,
Code Hint tool, as
preferred suffix
Script panel Code

4 Sav

Tilin

In this se
dynamica
this appro
graphic, w
your envir
enables you
different til
tication of y

This project uses two tiles to demonstrate how this concept works. The following figure shows an example of a reusable, tile-based background. You can find these tiles in the **Bonus** folder in the Library.

1   Open the Tree Maze scene. You'll notice that there is nothing on the Stage other than the Score text. The Timeline has two layers: scripts and score. The scripts layer has a folder that contains all the code neatly organized in five layers: initialize, sounds, functions, actions, and listener.

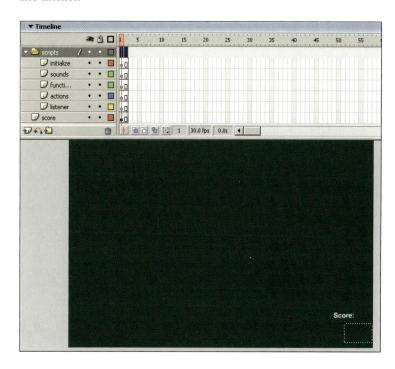

2 Go to the first frame of the initialize layer. Open the Actions panel and type this script:

Listing 5.2

```
//Initializing variables

_global.Tilewidth = 30;          //Tile width
_global.Tileheight = 30;         //Tile height

var mazeDepth:Number = 1000;     //Starting instance
                                 ➥level
var score:Number = 0;            //Starting score
var winScore:Number = 0;         //End score (defined in
                                 ➥map Array)
var obstacle:Number = 2;         //Variable to indicate
                                 ➥which elements are solid
var speed:Number = Tilewidth/3;  //Variable to indicate
                                 ➥player speed
```

This script declares seven variables that are used to build the maze: Tilewidth, Tileheight, mazeDepth, score, winScore, obstacle, and speed. Speed is defined as Tilewidth/3. If you want the character to move faster, try dividing the Tilewidth by 2 instead of 3.

Note: Identifying a variable as _global will make it visible to every Timeline in the movie. When using _global, do not use the variable declaration (var =) syntax.

You're using _global here because constants in Flash refer to built-in values such as those associated with the Key and Math classes. By using var to declare Timeline variables and strictly typing them, you are prevented from assigning the wrong type value to the variable.

---

3 Go to the actions layer. Add this script in the first frame:

Listing 5.3

```
//Create a container movie clip named 'cell' and make it
➥the movie's root

createEmptyMovieClip("cell", 1);
cell._x = Tilewidth;
cell._y = Tileheight;
cell._lockroot;
```

Here you create an empty movie clip through ActionScript to act as a container and define it as the root for the duration of this movie by using the _lockroot property.

Assigning cell's x and y values to variables allows you to change the size of the maze by modifying the values associated with Tilewidth and Tileheight.

4 Go to the functions layer. Enter this script in Frame 1:

Listing 5.4

```
/* Resource Functions */

//The addSprite function attaches instances of the sprite
➥name to the cell container.
function addSprite(sprite, mc_name, x, y) {
    cell.attachMovie(sprite, mc_name, mazeDepth--);
    cell[mc_name]._x = x*Tilewidth;
    cell[mc_name]._y = y*Tileheight;
}
```

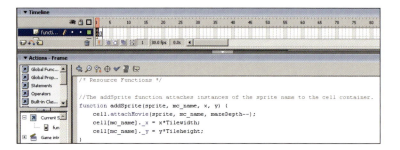

The function called addSprite takes four parameters: sprite, mc_name, x, and y. This function places all cells on the Stage, gives them a name, and assigns their _x and _y properties by multiplying x and y by the Tilewidth to position the movie clip. Depending on the order it is called will depend on what appears on top. In this version, puffin appears below the balloons. That can be changed either by placing the character on the Stage first or by changing the attachMovie parameter to mazeDepth++.

5   Now you are ready to create the map grid. In the actions layer, add this code to your script:

Listing 5.5

```
_global.map = [[2,2,2,2,2,2,2,2,2,2,2,2,2,2,2,2],
               [2,1,0,0,0,2,0,0,2,0,0,0,0,0,0,2],
               [2,0,2,2,0,2,0,2,0,2,2,2,2,2,0,2],
               [2,0,2,0,0,0,0,0,0,0,0,0,0,2,0,2],
               [2,0,0,0,0,2,0,0,2,0,2,0,0,0,0,2],
               [2,0,2,2,0,2,2,2,2,2,0,2,2,0,0,2],
               [2,0,0,0,2,0,0,0,2,0,0,0,2,0,0,2],
               [2,2,2,2,0,2,2,0,2,2,0,2,2,2,2,2],
               [2,0,0,0,2,0,0,0,0,0,0,0,2,0,0,2],
               [2,0,2,2,0,2,2,2,2,2,0,2,2,0,0,2],
               [2,0,0,0,0,2,0,2,0,2,0,0,0,0,0,2],
               [2,0,2,0,0,0,0,0,0,0,0,0,0,2,0,2],
               [2,0,2,0,2,2,0,2,0,2,2,2,0,0,0,2],
               [2,0,0,0,0,2,0,2,0,2,2,0,0,0,0,2],
               [2,2,2,2,2,2,2,2,2,2,2,2,2,2,2,2]];
```

Using an array, you map the maze grid cell by cell, where each number identifies a game element. This map array defines where trees, balloons, and the starting character are. These values will be used to place the character, make obstacles register as solid, and calculate the winning score. In other words, this is the "heart of the game."

6   You now need to add these functions. Go to the function layer and enter this script right after the addSprite() function:

Listing 5.6

```
//The to_tile function recalculates the x and y values
➥passed to it based on their position relative to a tile
➥on the stage.
function to_tile(x, y) {
    var tileX = Math.floor(x/Tilewidth);
    var tileY = Math.floor(y/Tileheight);
    return {x:tileX, y:tileY};
}

//The get_tile function, conversely, gets the identity of
➥the tile located at the x and y positions.
//(returning a value of either 0, 1 or 2)
function get_tile(x, y) {
    var tileX = Math.floor(x/Tilewidth);
    var tileY = Math.floor(y/Tileheight);
    return (map[tileY][tileX]);
}
```

The function to_tile() will be used to determine which tile the player's character is currently in. The function get_tile() will be used for collision detection with solid tiles (in this case, trees) to prevent the user from walking through them.

7   Right-click/Ctrl-click on the **tile** movie clip in the Library and assign the following Linkage properties:

Identifier: tile

Check: Export for ActionScript and Export in First Frame

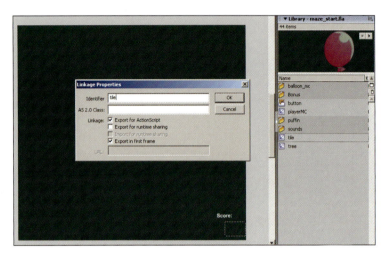

8   Go back to Frame 1 of the functions layer. Add a nested loop to populate the rows and columns of the maze grid. Then type this script:

Listing 5.7

```
function initTiles() {
    //Define the height and width of the maze by getting
    ➥the length of each array element.
    var height:Number = map.length;
    var width:Number = map[0].length;
    //This set of nested for loops builds the maze, looping
    ➥through the array and placing tiles on the stage,
    ➥then
    //assigning them values based on their position and
    ➥jumping to the proper display frame (either a balloon
    ➥or a tree).
    for (y=0; y<height; y++) {
        for (x=0; x<width; x++) {
            var mc_name = "t"+x+"_"+y;
            addSprite("tile", mc_name, x, y);
            cell[mc_name].p = to_tile(cell[mc_name]._x,
            ➥cell[mc_name]._y);
            cell[mc_name].gotoAndStop(map[y][x]+1);
            if (map[y][x] == 0) { winScore++; }
            if (map[y][x] == 1) { charLoc = [y, x]; }
        }
    }
}
```

The `initTiles()` function has two local variables named `height` and `width`, which are scoped to this function. The `mc_name` variable is created so that Flash does not have to calculate the values for the name multiple times during the loop.

The outer loop runs for as long as `y<height` of the maze (the number of rows in the map array) is `true`. The inner loop executes for as long as `x<width` (the number of columns in the map array) of maze.

The nested loop is dynamically creating the names of the tiles `t0_0`, `t0_1` through the total size of your array, which is `t14_14` in this case. (Remember: Although there are 15 rows and columns, the array begins at 0,0.) After a name is created, you create an instance of the `tile` movie clip inside the `cell` container sitting on the Stage.

Next there is a pair of if statements to check the current array value. If the array value is a balloon (0), the winScore variable will be incremented. This is the one you will check against to see if the player has gotten all of the balloons. If the array value is the player (1), you will generate a variable to use when we place the character in the maze.

The following figure shows what your code should look like at this point.

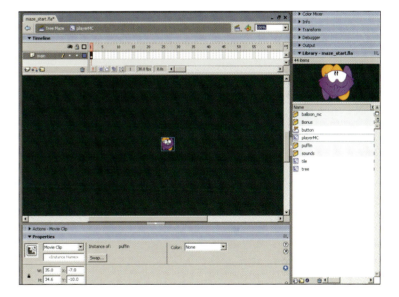

9   Save your work.

Collision Detection

At this stage in the project, with the environment built and balloons in place, it's time to display the main character and have a way to make it move. To do this, you'll create a new function called initPuffin. To get the character on the stage dynamically, you'll need to be able to access it from the Library. For this, you'll have to assign Linkage properties to the movie clip.

1   Open the Library and select the movie clip **playerMC** and double-click to go into Edit mode.

2   Select the movie clip playerMC on the Stage. Assign the instance name to playerMC: puffin_mc.

3   Select the playerMC in the Library. Then right-click/Ctrl-click and select Linkage. This launches the Linkage Properties panel. In the Identifier text field, type playerMC.

4 Select the Export for ActionScript and the Export in first frame
   options. Click OK.

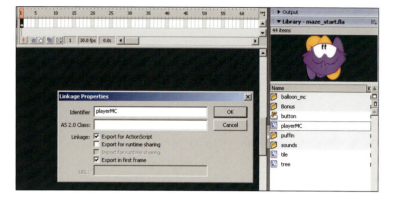

Now you'll write the script to display the character and allow the user
to manipulate it by using the arrow keys.

5 Navigate back to the Tree Maze main Timeline. Click on Frame 1 of
   the functions layer and add this script after the `initTiles()` function:

Listing 5.8

```
function initPuffin() {
//Place an instance of the playerMC on stage (given the
➥instance name 'player')
    addSprite("playerMC", "player", charLoc[0], charLoc[1]);
//Create the 'characterName' variable as a shortcut, to
➥reference the much longer nested name.
    _global.characterName = cell.player;
//Character stands still until the player presses a key.
    characterName.puffin_mc.gotoAndStop("still");
    inMotion = false;
//Define motion and collision detection variables.
//The bounds variable is referencing a built-in Movieclip
➥method to obtain 4 variables related to the character -
➥xMax, yMax, xMin, and yMin.
//The speed of the character is relative to the size of
➥the tiles
    bounds = characterName.getBounds(characterName);
}
```

The `addSprite()` function places an instance of the playerMC movie
clip from the Library onto the Stage in the top-left portion of the
maze, using the `charLoc` value you defined in the `initTiles` function.
Then, to save typing later on, you can create a variable named
`characterName` to store a reference to the `cell.player` path.

After the character is on the Stage, you'll want to pause the animation.
Otherwise, the puffin will be walking in place! You'll make the playhead advance to a frame in the animation where the puffin is standing
still, and create a variable to indicate its status.

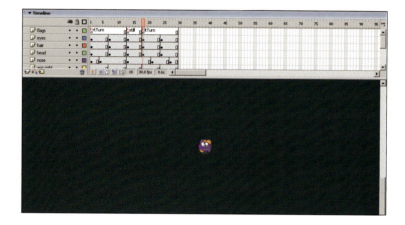

Note: For this game, you will write a math-based collision-detection
script. Rather than using the built-in `hitTest()` method, you will write a
script that calculates the position of the player against the bounds of
the tree tiles. This process provides far greater accuracy and flexibility,
which is also useful if you want to extend your game and add more
levels of complexity.

6   Enter the script here after the previous code on Frame 1 of the functions layer:

Listing 5.9

```
//The set_coords function is used for collision checking
➡against a tile.
function set_coords() {
    var a = to_tile(characterName._x, characterName._y);
    _global.playerc = {x:a.x, y:a.y};
}

//The move function is called whenever the player presses
➡(or holds) a key.
function mc_move(x, y, bounds) {
    var top = Math.floor(characterName._y+y);
    var bot = Math.floor(characterName._y+y+bounds.yMax/2);
    var lef = Math.floor(characterName._x+x);
    var rig = Math.floor(characterName._x+x+bounds.xMax/2);
    switch (obstacle) {
    case (get_tile(lef, top)) :
    case (get_tile(lef, bot)) :
    case (get_tile(rig, top)) :
    case (get_tile(rig, bot)) :
        break;
    default :
        characterName._x += x;
        characterName._y += y;
        break;
    }
}
```

The set_coords() function will take the current x and y location of the player on stage and translate that to an array position using the to_tile() function. This will then be assigned to a global variable so that it can be used in other timelines.

The mc_move() function determines the boundaries of the character and compares these to the array value of its current tile and the tile it is moving toward. The switch statement will not execute if the player character is colliding with an obstacle (if its current position in the array is equal to 2). Otherwise it will move in the direction of the values passed to the function.

A break statement is used to end execution of the case. Here, multiple case statements are nested to make sure that all of the conditions are met; otherwise, the default action is carried out.

The following figure shows what your code should look like at this point.

Note: Because the new version of Flash is more strongly typed than older versions, you must use the proper format when calling the xMax and yMax variables, variables which were created by the getBounds method in the initPuffin() function, by capitalizing the letter *M*. Not doing so would be perfectly acceptable in previous versions of Flash (including Flash MX), but will cause the motion to fail in this version.

7   Go to the actions layer. Type in the following statements right after the map Array:

Listing 5.10

```
//Place the tiles
initTiles();

//Define the player character
initPuffin();
```

Finally, the initialization functions are called once, when the game begins.

8   Save your work.

Character Movement

You can move the character in two ways: by checking for user interactions every time the playhead advances a frame (30 times per second in the case of this game), or by using listeners, which are more processor-friendly. Let's look at the Key Listener code.

Note: All input devices can have a listener in Flash. The mouse and keyboard objects both have methods to determine when the user is interacting with them. Listeners can also determine when the Stage has been resized, when a text field's content has changed, or when the user's cursor has changed focus.

1   Go to the first frame of the listener layer and type this script:

Listing 5.11

```
//Create a listener for keypresses.
onKeyDown = function () {
// Use Switch to check for four possible valid key presses
    switch (Key.getCode()) {
    case Key.UP :
        characterName.puffin_mc._rotation = 0;
        if (inMotion == false) {
characterName.puffin_mc.gotoAndPlay("rtTurn");      }
        inMotion = true;
        mc_move(0, -speed, bounds);
        collision(playerc.x, playerc.y);
        break;
```

The Key listener that is being used here is a method that executes whenever a key is pressed, regardless of the user's focus.

Note: Using listeners saves computer cycles and speeds up the game by only running character animation routines and collision detection while the user is pressing a key.

The switch statement replaces multiple if-else commands, retrieving the code of the key pressed by the user and comparing it to four potential values (UP, RIGHT, DOWN, and LEFT). You must type these directions in caps because they are Key object constants that correlate to the numerical values of the keys.

2   Type the following code right after the break; statement:

Listing 5.12

```
    case Key.RIGHT :
        characterName.puffin_mc._rotation = 90;
        if (inMotion == false) {
characterName.puffin_mc.gotoAndPlay("rtTurn");     }
        inMotion = true;
        mc_move(speed, 0, bounds);
        collision(playerc.x, playerc.y);
        break;
    case Key.DOWN :
        characterName.puffin_mc._rotation = 180;
        if (inMotion == false) {
characterName.puffin_mc.gotoAndPlay("ltTurn"); }
        inMotion = true;
        mc_move(0, speed, bounds);
        collision(playerc.x, playerc.y);
        break;
```

The line of code characterName.puffin._rotation = 0; and the one that follows it animate the character—turning it in the proper direction based on the arrow key being pressed, and beginning the walking animation while the key remains pressed. These actions send the puffin movie clip to various frame labels that control its motion.

The puffin avatar has three frame labels: ltTurn, still, and rtTurn.

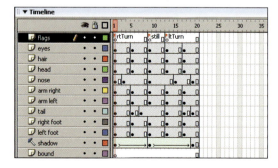

Remember: The `characterName` variable is just a reference to the longer `cell.player` path.

3 Pass the proper direction variables so that the character moves when the user presses one of the arrow keys. Insert this script right after the last `break;` statement:

Listing 5.13

```
    case Key.LEFT :
        characterName.puffin_mc._rotation = 270;
        if (inMotion == false) {
characterName.puffin_mc.gotoAndPlay("ltTurn");       }
        inMotion = true;
        mc_move(-speed, 0, bounds);
        collision(playerc.x, playerc.y);
        break;
        default :
        trace("no case tested true");
    }
// After the proper motion has been processed, reset the
➥coords position so the collision detection can take place
➥on the next keypress.
    set_coords();
};

//onKeyUp tell the character to stop its walking animation
onKeyUp = function () {
    characterName.puffin_mc.gotoAndStop("still");
    inMotion = false;
};
Key.addListener(this);
```

This code calls the `move()` function and passes variables in the proper direction to make the character move. The distance covered is based on the speed variable. The position of the speed parameter in this `move` function is based on the motion direction; a positive speed value in the x position moves right, and a positive speed value in the y position moves down. The respective negative values move up and left. The `break` command exits the switch command and allows the Flash player to check for a new key press.

Each time a key is pressed, the variables record the position of the puffin on the Stage.

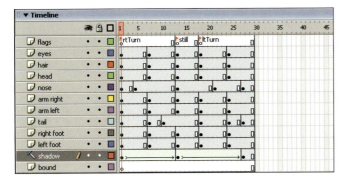

The following figure shows the code for the Listener layer.

```
//Create a listener for keypresses.
onKeyDown = function () {
    // Use Switch to check for four possible valid key presses
    switch (Key.getCode()) {
    case Key.UP :
        characterName.puffin_mc._rotation = 0;
        if (inMotion == false) { characterName.puffin_mc.gotoAndPlay("rtTurn"); }
        inMotion = true;
        mc_move(0, -speed, bounds);
        collision(playerc.x, playerc.y);
        break;
    case Key.RIGHT :
        characterName.puffin_mc._rotation = 90;
        if (inMotion == false) { characterName.puffin_mc.gotoAndPlay("rtTurn"); }
        inMotion = true;
        mc_move(speed, 0, bounds);
        collision(playerc.x, playerc.y);
        break;
    case Key.DOWN :
        characterName.puffin_mc._rotation = 180;
        if (inMotion == false) { characterName.puffin_mc.gotoAndPlay("ltTurn"); }
        inMotion = true;
        inMotion = true;
        mc_move(0, speed, bounds);
        collision(playerc.x, playerc.y);
        break;
    case Key.LEFT :
        characterName.puffin_mc._rotation = 270;
        if (inMotion == false) { characterName.puffin_mc.gotoAndPlay("ltTurn"); }
        inMotion = true;
        mc_move(-speed, 0, bounds);
        collision(playerc.x, playerc.y);
        break;
    default :
        trace("no case tested true");
    }
    // After the proper motion has been proccessed, reset the coords position so the collision detection can to
    set_coords();
};

//onKeyUp tell the character to stop it's walking animation
onKeyUp = function () {
    characterName.puffin_mc.gotoAndStop("still");
    inMotion = false;
};
Key.addListener(this);
```

The much shorter onKeyUp function stops all character animation except for the blinking eyes and alerts the Flash player to the fact that the character is no longer in motion. You have to keep track of the motion status of the puffin; otherwise, it would either play the walk animation constantly or never display it at all.

Now that you have defined the methods for the motionListener object, you can assign this object to the Key listener.

Now whenever the player presses an arrow key, the character moves through the forest.

5   Save your work.

Adding Sounds

Using sound in games goes beyond aesthetics; sound has a purpose. It provides feedback to your user when he is interacting with your game. Sound is a key element to successful game development and design.

For this project, you will use two sound effects that you will pull from the Library using ActionScript. One is triggered each time the character collects a balloon, and the other one is triggered when the game is over. The two sounds are located in the Sounds folder in the Library and are called: **grab** and **done**.

1   Right-click/Ctrl-click on the **grab** sound and select Linkage.

2   Select the Export for ActionScript and the Export in First Frame options. In the Linkage Properties panel, type the identifier name <u>grab</u>.

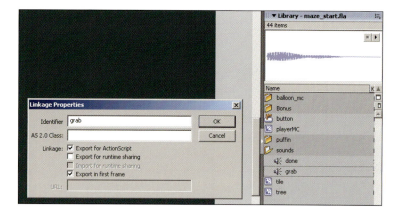

3   Repeat Step 2 for the **done** sound effect. In the Linkage Properties panel, type the identifier name <u>done</u>.

4 Go to the first frame in the sounds layer and open the Actions panel. Add the following script:

Listing 5.14

```
//The sounds layer creates two new sound objects,
//"grab" and "done", and attaches linked sounds
//from the library.

var grab_sound:Sound = new Sound();
var done_sound:Sound = new Sound();
grab_sound.attachSound("grab");
done_sound.attachSound("done");
```

This script pulls the two sounds from the Library and attaches each one to a sound object using `attachSound()`. This method offers more control and flexibility (as opposed to placing each sound on a frame). You can now manipulate the sounds using the methods and properties of the Sound object and call them anywhere in the movie, as demonstrated in the next section.

Once again, adding the suffix `_sound` will reference the properties of the built-in Sound object in the Code Hints panel.

5 Save your work.

Keeping Score

Keeping score is an effective way of displaying a user's progress throughout the game. This section introduces the concept of scoring in Flash. You will use the dynamic text box on Stage to build the scoring feature of the maze.

1 Click on the dynamic text box on Stage under the text Score. Using the Properties panel, enter the variable value <u>score</u> and the instance name <u>display</u>.

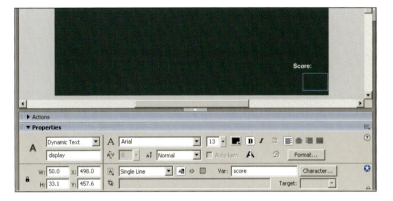

2 Click on Frame 1 of the functions layer. Enter this script on Frame 1 right after the `mc_move()` function:

Listing 5.15

```
function collision(x, y) {
    var mc_name = "t"+x+"_"+y;
    if (cell[mc_name].p.x == x && cell[mc_name].p.y =
➥= y && cell[mc_name]._currentframe == 1) {
        grab_sound.start();
        score++;
        //If the player has grabbed all of the balloons,
        ➥then they win and the victory sound "done" plays.
        if (score>=winScore) {
            score = "YAY";
            //gotoAndStop("done");
            done_sound.start();
        }
        //Removing the movie clip will leave an empty space
        ➥on the stage where the balloon once was.
        removeMovieClip(cell[mc_name]);
    }
}
```

Here, you create a loop that checks whether the puffin picked up a balloon as the user moved him around the maze. The current tile is being checked each time an arrow key is pressed. If all the balloons are picked, then the user has won and the done sound can start playing.

If the puffin is in a tile that contains a balloon, you will make the balloon disappear, play the sound grab sound, and add a point to the user's score, as shown in the following two lines from Listing 5.15.

```
grab sound.start();
score++;
```

The score is updated directly in the text field you just created.

If the score is equal to the total number of balloons (the variable winScore), the user will have won the game, in which case you will play the done sound.

At this point, you will change the message in the Score box. Otherwise, the player would be stuck wandering around an empty playing field.

```
removeMovieClip(cell[mc_name]);
```

When a balloon has been obtained and a point added to the score, you can remove the tile movie clip instance from the Stage.

```
(removeMovieClip(_root.cell[name]);).
```

3 Now run the movie and see how it works. Move the puffin around the maze using your arrow keys. Feel free to adjust the speed if you think he's moving too fast or too slow.

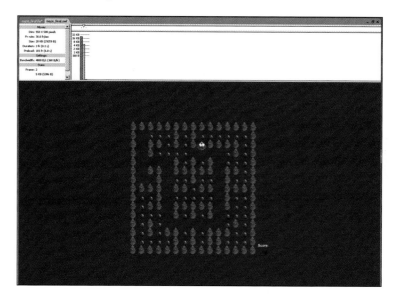

4 Save your work. Well done! You just built a full-blown maze game and kept it under 25Kb.

Now Try This

In this project, you've learned many skills and techniques for building games, including how to script motion Listeners and collision detectors. You've also added sound and created a score keeper. Of course, this is only the beginning.

Here are some ideas on how to apply the skills you've learned or use the project you've completed in other ways:

- Using the concepts discussed in this project, you can extend the maze by adding more levels. A **Bonus** folder that has more tiles you can use is included in the movie Library. Feel free to experiment.

- Try adding another character—perhaps an opponent—or use a timer that counts down while the user is trying to catch all the balloons.

- Tile-based games offer great flexibility through the reuse of graphical assets. You can take full advantage of that by using external files (XML, .txt) to load data into Flash and generate more complex environments.

Creating a Navigable 3D Environment with ActionScript 2 Classes

Chad Corbin

Chad Corbin
is an award-winning Flash developer who is best known for his work on lo9ic.com. Currently, Chad works for Wall Street On Demand, where he develops Flash applications and financial websites for leading investment firms.

Even though I browse the Internet every day and make a living building interactive sites, I feel like there is something missing from whole web experience. Day in and day out, my only interaction with sites is point and click, point and click, point and, well, you get the idea. There has to be a better way.

Why not make sites that mimic life, where we can walk around and interact with the objects we encounter? Why are we constrained to scrolling page after page when applications like Flash allow us to create new ways to experience the web? Perhaps I'm never one to be content, but then again, I'll never know if I don't at least try. It's the process of trying something new or taking on a difficult challenge that makes all this stuff interesting, and luckily for me, that's exactly what I get to do when I work on projects like this.

It Works Like This

You will be creating a simple, navigable 3D environment by writing your own ActionScript 2 classes. When the project is finished, you will be able to move around within multiple 3D scenes using the keyboard, view information about the objects you approach, and jump from scene to scene. Here are the basic steps of the project:

1 Write the custom classes for each object in the movie, starting with the `Generic` class. The `Generic` class includes functions for moving and scaling the objects.

2 Write the `Clip`, `Camera`, and `Scene` classes, which will manage the assets and settings of the 3D scene.

3 Write the 3D classes (`Quaternion` and `Node`) to handle all the mathematical calculations.

4 Create the visual assets of the movie (in the form of movie clips) and incorporate the classes into an FLA using the methods and properties written in steps 1–3.

5 Add interaction to the project with a function that listens to keystrokes and creates movement in the 3D scene.

Use custom and 3D classes to create a navigable 3D environment.

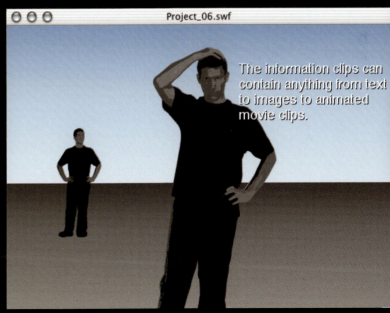

The information clips can contain anything from text to images to animated movie clips.

This 3D environment can be used in immersive websites and games.

Preparing to Work

To prepare for this project, you will need to do the following:

1   Copy the **Projects/06** folder to your hard drive.

Note: A complete copy of the finished files and directory structure is included on the CD; however, you should only use these files for reference. You will get more out of the project if you create and code the files yourself rather than simply looking at and compiling the examples.

---

2   Open the **Project_06.swf** file from the **Projects/06/Project_06_src** folder. Using the arrows on the keypad, take a few minutes to see how the finished project will look and function. This is exactly what you will be building.

3   Create a directory on your hard disk named Project_06.

This is where you will put the FLA that you will create later.

Note: It is common practice to place class files into directories that mirror the structure of the program and relationship between the classes. For example, if you were building an application that used several classes to construct a scrollbar, you might set up the directory structure to be: **myapplication/scrollbar/**. Although it might seem unnecessary, the directory structure can help to organize your code, especially when you need to create many different classes.

---

4   Within the **Project_06** directory, create another directory and name it F3D.

This is where you will place the class files that you write.

5   Within the **F3D** directory, create a directory named **Math**.

This directory will contain the 3D Math class.

6   Open your preferred text editor so that you can use the it to write the class files for this project.

If you are using Flash MX Professional 2004, you can use the built-in code editor to create the class files. You must choose File > New and select ActionScript File to launch a new .as file in the included editor.

Note: Although classes and objects are sometimes used interchangeably, they actually refer to slightly different concepts. *Classes* are templates for creating objects, but classes by themselves do not constitute objects. However, after an instance of a class is created, the instance is an *object*.

Note: Generally speaking, you never want to refer to an object's variables directly. Instead, create `getter` and `setter` functions that modify the value of the variables you are interested in accessing. This allows you to restructure and change the name of variables within a class without having to recode each external reference to the variables.

Note: ActionScript 2.0 contains many new enhancements including class-based syntax, strong variable typing, interfaces and packages. More information about ActionScript 2.0 can be found on the Macromedia website at `http://www.macromedia.com/devnet/mx/flash/actionscript.html`

Creating the *Generic* Class

The Generic class will be the basis for another class that you will write later. The purpose of this class is to define common methods from which other classes can inherit. In this project, the Clip class inherits methods from Generic.

Here, the Generic class definition defines a member variable (clip), the class constructor function (Generic()), and the moveTo() and scaleTo() functions that move and scale the object referenced by the clip variable. The latter two functions are called later in the project to move and scale the people in the scene.

Note: A finished copy of this class is saved as **Generic.as** in the **Project_06_scr/F3D** directory.

---

1 With a text editor, create a new document and save it in the **Project_06/F3D** folder as Generic.as.

2 At the top of the file, add this block of code:

Listing 6.1

```
class F3D.Generic {
    public var clip:MovieClip;
    function Generic(ca:MovieClip) {
        clip = ca;
    }
    public function moveTo(x:Number, y:Number):Void {
        clip._x = x;
        clip._y = y;
    }
    public function scaleTo(xs:Number, ys:Number):Void {
        clip._xscale = xs;
        clip._yscale = ys;
    }
}
```

Why did you name the class F3D.Generic? For the Flash compiler to know where a class is located, you must supply a fully qualified class name that includes the class path. Because you saved the file in the F3D directory, the class path is F3D and the class name is Generic, and the fully qualified name is F3D.Generic. All the classes within this directory must have F3D at the beginning.

Note that the keyword class is required by the compiler to tell it that this is a class definition.

Note: Class files define the member functions and variables that are associated with a particular class of objects. In Flash, only one class can be defined per file.

---

3 Save your work and close the file.

Creating the *Clip* Class to Manage Visual Assets

In this section, you'll script the Clip class definition, extending the Generic class that was created previously. In the 3D environment, clips are used to manage the objects in the scene. Each clip references a movie clip that is attached to the Stage. As you move through the scene, the draw function positions and scales the clip based on the values in node and Camera using a 3D to 2D perspective transformation. When the clip is drawn in certain positions, it can display a movie clip within the attached clip, or transport you to a different scene. In the finished project, the Clip class is used to create the people in the scene.

Note: Figuring out how to structure classes can be tricky. When coding your own classes, take the time to figure out what methods and variables will be needed before you start to type. This will result in well-designed classes that can be reused or extended for make more specialized purposes.

Note: Refer to **Clip.as** in the **Project_06_scr/F3D** directory for a completed version.

1   Create a new file with your text editor.

2   At the top of the file, add this block of code:

Listing 6.2

```
import F3D.Node;
import F3D.Generic;
import F3D.Camera;

class F3D.Clip extends Generic {
    public var node:Node;
    public var link:String;
    public var info:String;
    public var callback:Function;
    private var zfactor:Number;
    public function Clip(ca:MovieClip) {
        super(ca);
    }
    public function draw():Void {
        if (node.z <0) {
            zfactor = 1-node.z/Camera.f;
            moveTo(Math.round(node.x/zfactor), Math.round
            ➥(node.y/zfactor));
            scaleTo(Math.round(1/zfactor*100), Math.round
            ➥(1/zfactor*100));
            clip.swapDepths(Math.round(1000000-Math.abs
            ➥(node.z*100)));
            clip._visible = true;
            if (node.x < 50 && node.x > -50 && node.z >
            ➥ -20 && link) {
                callback(link);
            } else if (node.x < 50 && node.x > -50 && node.z
            ➥ > -100 && info) {
                clip[info]._visible = true;
            } else if (info && clip[info]) {
                clip[info]._visible = false;
            }
        } else {
            clip._visible = false;
        }
    }
}
```

Because this class uses other classes in its definition, you have to use the import statement at the top of the file. This statement tells the compiler where to find the definitions of the classes referenced in this file. Just like naming classes, you have to use a fully qualified class name when using import.

Notice that the Clip class extends the Generic class that you wrote previously. This means that it inherits all the variable and function definitions of Generic. This new feature of ActionScript 2 allows you to reuse classes and organize code in a logical way. You could have created Clip without extending Generic just by putting the code from Generic into Clip. However, extending classes is a good technique to learn, so it is included here.

Note: Constructor functions take the same name as the class in which they reside. A *constructor function* tells the compiler what code to execute within an instance whenever a new instance is created. Often-times, the constructor takes arguments that initialize instance variables. Constructor functions are required; however, if left out, the compiler automatically inserts an empty constructor for you.

3   Save the file as Clip.as in **the Project_06/F3D** folder.

Creating the *Camera* Class to Store a Global Variable

The Camera class acts as a global object. You will never actually create instances from the class; instead, you will refer directly to the class to get the property f.

Note: A complete example is included in the **Project_06_scr/F3D** directory.

When you define a class, both the class and its members are globally accessible to the rest of your code. This allows you to reference the class from any instance or function without having to pass a pointer to each object that uses the class.

1   With your text editor, create a new document and save it in the **Project_06/F3D** folder as <u>Camera.as</u>.

2   At the top of the file, add this block of code:

Listing 6.3

```
class F3D.Camera {
    static public var f:Number = 300;
}
```

The Camera class is always referenced by its uppercase class name.

The static declaration tells the compiler to create pointers to the static variables and member functions of the class rather than create new variables and member functions for each instance. This allows you to access values and functions within the scope of the class instead of the instance, making it possible to share the same variables and functions across all instances created from the class.

3   Save your work and close the file.

Creating the *Scene* Class to Manage Scene Properties

Now it is time to write the Scene class definition. The Scene class will allow you to create different scenes in the 3D environment. Scenes will be composed of a background (referenced by the background property) and elements (referenced in the elements array). Each element contains the name of the movie clip to attach, the node associated with the clip, a link property, and an info property.

Note: The **Scene.as** file included in the **Project_06_scr/F3D** directory shows the completed code.

The latter two properties determine the behavior of the element in the scene. The link property, when set, is the name of another scene. This allows you to link from scene to scene as you move through the environment. The info property, when set, is the name of a movie clip within the elements. When the attached clip is in certain positions onscreen, the movie clip referenced by the info property appears. In the example SWF, the scene is everything you see onscreen, including the people and the background.

1   With your text editor, create a new document.

2   At the top of the file, add this block of code:

Listing 6.4

```
import F3D.Node;
class F3D.Scene {
    public var elements:Array;
    public var background:String;
    function Scene() {
        elements = new Array()
    }
    public function addElement(c:String, n:Node, l:String,
i:String):Void {
        elements.push({clip:c, node:n, link:l, info:i});
    }
    public function setBackground(b:String):Void {
        background = b;
    }
}
```

The Scene class allows you to create different scenes within the 3D environment, each looking and behaving differently. Note that "scene" in this case does not refer to the different scenes that you can create with the Flash Timeline.

Note: ActionScript 2 supports strong typing of variables. Strongly typed variables allow you to create code that is easier to read and helps the compiler catch errors that could take hours to find when debugging by hand. The syntax `var myVar:myClass = new myClass()` might look familiar from other programming languages.

3 Save the file as <u>Scene.as</u> in the **Project_06/F3D** folder.

Creating the *Quaternion* Class to Rotate Objects in the Scene

With the basic classes out of the way, it's time to focus on the 3D engine. In these steps, you'll write `Quaternion` and `Node` classes to do all the 3D calculations. The theory behind these calculations is beyond the scope of this project, so you might not completely understand how they work when you are finished writing their code. However, after you've written the classes, you can reuse them in almost any 3D project you create in the future.

Of all the classes you have written so far, this is perhaps the hardest to conceptualize. Quaternions are four-dimensional vectors that contain position and orientation information encoded in four components: x, y, z, and w. In 3D engines, Quaternions are used to keep track of the position and rotation of objects in space. Because of the relative small size and low number of calculations required as compared to other methods, Quaternions can be fast and efficient in 3D engines.

Note: A *Quaternion* is a mathematical concept that represents an orientation with four variables. In a basic sense, a Quaternion defines an axis and angle of rotation. When two Quaternions are concatenated, the resulting Quaternion is a rotation of one by the other. Thus, a Quaternion can be used to rotate other Quaternions in space. When points are expanded into a Quaternion notation, they, too, can be rotated in space.

Note: Later in the project, you will write code that calls these methods to rotate the scene. Please refer to **Quaternion.as** in the **Project_06_src/F3D/Math** folder for the completed code.

1 Start by creating a new document with your text editor.

2 At the top of the file, add the following block of code:

Listing 6.5

```
class F3D.Math.Quaternion {
    public var x, y, z, w :Number;
    function Quaternion(xa:Number, ya:Number, za:Number,
    ➥wa:Number) {
        x = xa != null ? xa : 0;
        y = ya != null ? ya : 0;
        z = za != null ? za : 0;
        w = wa != null ? wa : 1;
    }
    public function rotateY(theta:Number):Void {
        var halfangle:Number = (theta*Math.PI/180)/2;
        x = 0;
        y = Math.sin(halfangle);
        z = 0;
        w = Math.cos(halfangle);
    }
    public function concatenate(qa:Quaternion):Void {
        var xt:Number = x;
        var yt:Number = y;
        var zt:Number = z;
        var wt:Number = w;
        x = wt*qa.x + xt*qa.w + zt*qa.y - yt*qa.z;
        y = wt*qa.y + yt*qa.w + xt*qa.z - zt*qa.x;
        z = wt*qa.z + zt*qa.w + yt*qa.x - xt*qa.y;
        w = wt*qa.w - xt*qa.x - yt*qa.y - zt*qa.z;
    }
    public function invert():Void {
        x = -x;
        y = -y;
        z = -z;
    }
    public function duplicate():Quaternion {
        return new Quaternion(x, y, z, w);
    }
}
```

In this project, a Quaternion is used to rotate the people in the 3D scene. Think of it as the mathematical equivalent to standing in place and turning left or right. The Quaternion class has four member functions:

rotateY()	Resets the Quaternion to rotate theta degrees about the y axis of the scene. You will use rotateY() in the main script of the FLA.
concatenate()	Takes the Quaternion and rotates it around the Quaternion passed as an argument. This function rotated all the Nodes (yet to be created) in the scene.
invert()	Reverses the direction of the Quaternion. invert() is used in the rotation calculation.
duplicate()	Returns a new copy of the Quaternion. It's also used in the rotation calculation.

Note: Just like variables, functions can be typed. The function type in ActionScript 2 is based on the type of the return value. Functions that do not return a value should be of type Void.

3 Save the file as Quaternion.as in the Project_06/F3D/Math folder.

Creating the *Node* Class to Define Positions in 3D Space

This class will be the basic element of the 3D environment. Having x, y, and z properties, this class defines a point in 3D space. In addition to position properties, the Node class has member functions rotate() and translate() that rotate and translate the point in space.

Nodes are commonly used in 3D engines to optimize the number of 3D points that have to be calculated. For instance, if you were to create a 3D cube, you would need to define six polygons, each with four corners. If you were to calculate the position of each corner individually, you would have to perform 24 separate calculations. If instead you allowed the polygons to share corners using nodes, you cut the number of 3D calculations down to eight, significantly increasing the efficiency of the engine.

Note: Refer to **Node.as** in the **Project_06_src/F3D** directory for the finished class definition.

1 Use your text editor to create a new document and save it in the Project_06/F3D folder as Node.as.

2 At the top of the file, add this block of code:

Listing 6.6

```
import F3D.Math.Quaternion;
class F3D.Node {
    public var x, y, z :Number;
    private var qt, ri :Quaternion;
    static var nodes:Array = new Array();
    public function Node(xa:Number, ya:Number, za:Number) {
        x = xa != null ? xa : 0;
        y = ya != null ? ya : 0;
        z = za != null ? za : 0;
        nodes.push(this);
    }
    public function rotate(ra:Quaternion):Void {
        qt = new Quaternion(x, y, z, 0);
        ri = ra.duplicate();
        ri.invert();
        qt.concatenate(ra);
        ri.concatenate(qt);
        x = ri.x;
        y = ri.y;
        z = ri.z;
    }
    public function translate(xa:Number, ya:Number,
    ➥za:Number):Void {
        x += xa;
        y += ya;
        z += za;
    }
}
```

The public and private keywords tell the compiler to allow or restrict access to class and instance members. Variables and functions that are declared as public are accessible by any object in the script. On the other hand, variables and members that are declared as private can only be accessed from within the class or instance. Use the keyword public when you want other classes to be able to call variables and methods within the class. Use private when the variable and function is used only within the class and never needs to be called except by methods within the class.

The functions rotate() and translate() modify the position of the node in space.

3   Save the file and close it.

Creating the People and Background Assets

Now that you have created the class, you are going to switch gears and create movie clips to go into the 3D scenes. You can place any image or drawn art into the clips, but keep in mind that although the 3D engine will move and scale the movie clips, it will not rotate the images inside. These movie clips will become the people and backgrounds in the completed project.

Note: A completed FLA is located in the **Project_06_src** directory on the CD.

Note: You will notice that as the complexity of the images used increases; the performance of the movie will decrease. You may have to experiment with several images to find the right balance of imagery that looks good and still allows the movie to run smoothly.

1   Create a new FLA and save the file in the Project_06 folder as Project_06.fla.

2   Open the Library palette in Flash by choosing Ctrl/Cmd+L.

3   Click the + button at the bottom to create a new movie clip.

4   Name the clip person_1 and check the Export for ActionScript and Export in First Frame check boxes. Make sure to enter person_1 as the export name for the clip.

5   Place drawn or imported images into the clip. When placing images, make sure that the bottom edge of the image aligns with the registration point and center the image horizontally.

If you prefer, you can use the images used in the example FLA included on the CD. Open the example FLA Library and copy an image from one of the Library items: **person_1**, **person_2**, or **person_3**.

6   If you want the clip to contain an information clip, create a new movie clip within the current clip on a layer above the image, name it info, and place the content that you want to appear into the new clip.

Remember that this info clip will become visible whenever the parent clip is at the center of the scene.

The information clips can contain anything from text to images to animated movie clips.

7   Repeat Steps 3-6 several times to create several movie clips. Name each person incrementally.

8   Click the + button at the bottom of the Library palette to begin making the background clips for the scene.

9   Again, place drawn or imported images into the clip. This time, however, use an image that makes a suitable background. Make sure that the background image is centered both vertically and horizontally.

10 Name the first background background_1 and increment the number for subsequent clips. Just like the previous clips, make sure that these have export names and export settings checked.

Background images are centered in the movie clip and should be at least as large as the Stage.

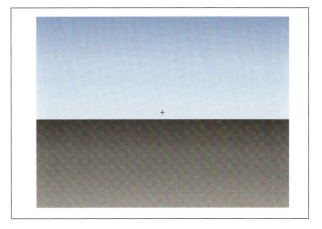

11 Repeat the preceding steps until you have several backgrounds.

12 Save your work.

Integrating the Classes with the FLA

With all the classes written and all the assets created, it is time to write the main movie script. In these steps, you will write ActionScript that imports classes, initializes global variables, and creates 3D scenes.

1   Go back to Scene 1 within the **Project_06.fla** file that you created in the previous section.

2 Click the first frame of the movie, open the Actions window (F9), and add this code to the frame:

Listing 6.7

```
import F3D.Math.Quaternion;
import F3D.*;
var container:MovieClip ;
var manager:Object ;
var r:Quaternion;
var myInt:Number;
var scene1:Scene = new Scene();
var scene2:Scene = new Scene();
var scene3:Scene = new Scene();
```

Just as in class definitions, you must import classes into the FLA using the `import` statement. The next statements import the `Quaternion` class and all classes in the **F3D** folder. Note that the wildcard, *, can be used to import a group of classes without listing each individually. Below the `import` statement are the variable declarations for the main script.

Even if the values of the variables are not set initially, it is good practice to declare and type each variable at the top of the script.

Note: In the past, writing `var MyVar = 2` was equivalent to writing `var myvar = 2`. In ActionScript 2, however, the two statements are not equivalent because AS2 is case-sensitive.

3 Insert this code to define the scenes:

Listing 6.8

```
scene1.setBackground("background1");
scene1.addElement("clip1", new Node(1000, 0, 200),
➥"scene2", null);
scene1.addElement("clip1", new Node(2000, 0, 0),
➥"scene2", null);
scene1.addElement("clip1", new Node(1000, 0, -200),
➥"scene2", null);
scene2.setBackground("background2");
scene2.addElement("clip2", new Node(-500, 0, 1000),
➥"scene3", null);
scene2.addElement("clip2", new Node(-500, 0, 0), null,
➥"info");
scene2.addElement("clip2", new Node(-500, 0, -1000),
➥"scene3", null);
scene3.setBackground("background3");
scene3.addElement("clip3", new Node(500, 0, 1000),
➥"scene1", null);
scene3.addElement("clip3", new Node(500, 0, 0), "scene1",
➥null);
scene3.addElement("clip3", new Node(500, 0, -1000),
➥"scene1", null);
```

This section of code defines the movie clips that are to appear in each scene, their properties, and the node to which they are attached. The scenes and clip names shown here differ slightly from the ones in the example FLA.

4 For each line in the code that contains `setBackground`, substitute the exported name of a background clip in the Library.

5 In all other lines of this section, substitute the exported names of the clips that are to appear in the scene. For example, substitute background1 with background_1, clip1 with person_1, and so on. If you want the clip to link you to a different scene, enter a scene name in the third parameter; otherwise, the parameter should be `null`. Likewise, if the exported clip contains an info clip, you must pass the name of the info clip in the last parameter.

6   To be able to jump from scene to scene, you have to add functions that clear and create scenes. To do this, insert these functions at the end of the script:

Listing 6.9

```
function swapScene (s) {
    clearScene();
    makeScene(s);
}
function clearScene() {
    container = _root.createEmptyMovieClip("containermc",
    ➥1);
    container._x = 275;
    container._y = 200;
    manager = new Object();
    AsBroadcaster.initialize(manager);
    r = new Quaternion();
}
function makeScene(s) {
    clearInterval(myInt);
    var i:Number = 0;
    for (i in this[s].elements) {
        var n:Node = this[s].elements[i].node;
        var bg:MovieClip = container.attachMovie(this[s].
        ➥background, "background", 1);
        var mc:MovieClip = container.attachMovie(this[s].
        ➥elements[i].clip, s +"_clip_"+i, i+2);
        var c:Clip = new Clip(mc);
        mc._visible = false;
        c.node = n;
        c.link = this[s].elements[i].link;
        c.info = this[s].elements[i].info ?
        ➥this[s].elements[i].info : null;
        c.callback = swapScene;
        manager.addListener(n);
        manager.addListener(c);
    }
    myInt = setInterval(run, 10);
}
```

These functions allow you to dynamically swap the 3D scene. The function clearScene() initializes the movie by creating a container clip and centering it on stage. The function also creates an object called manager that will broadcast the rotate, translate, and draw events to the clip objects in the scene. Using AsBroadcaster to broadcast messages is much more efficient than looping through all of the objects and drawing them individually.

MakeScene() takes the scene and creates a clip object from each element, assigning the attributes defined by the element, and adding it and its node as listeners to the manager. Finally, the function calls setInterval to begin execution of run(), a function that you will write next.

7   Save your work.

Triggering Movement in the Scene with Key Commands

The scripting is almost complete; only one function is left to write. The basic idea of this function is to wire in the keyboard so that certain keys trigger movement through the 3D scene. The run() function checks which keys are depressed and broadcasts the translate or rotate messages to the listening objects.

1   Below the last line of code in the FLA, add this function:

Listing 6.10

```
function run() {
    if (Key.isDown(Key.UP) && !Key.isDown(Key.SPACE)) {
        manager.broadcastMessage("translate",0,0,10);
    } else if (Key.isDown(Key.DOWN) && !Key.isDown
➡(Key.SPACE)) {
        manager.broadcastMessage("translate",0,0,-10);
    }
    if (Key.isDown(Key.RIGHT) && !Key.isDown(Key.SPACE)) {
        r.rotateY(1);
        manager.broadcastMessage("rotate",r);
    } else if (Key.isDown(Key.LEFT) && !Key.isDown
➡(Key.SPACE)) {
        r.rotateY(-1);
        manager.broadcastMessage("rotate",r);
    }
    if (Key.isDown(Key.RIGHT) && Key.isDown(Key.SPACE)) {
        manager.broadcastMessage("translate",-10,0,0);
    } else if (Key.isDown(Key.LEFT) && Key.isDown
➡(Key.SPACE)) {
        manager.broadcastMessage("translate",10,0,0);
    }
    if (Key.isDown(Key.LEFT) || Key.isDown(Key.RIGHT) ||
➡Key.isDown(Key.UP) || Key.isDown(Key.DOWN)) {
        manager.broadcastMessage("draw");
    }
}
```

When the movie is running, pressing the up arrow key moves you forward in the scene, and pressing the down arrow key moves you back. Holding the right and left arrows rotates the scene, while holding the left or right arrow along with the spacebar slides the scene left and right.

2   Finally, add two lines of code to set and draw the default scene:

Listing 6.11

```
swapScene("scene1");
manager.broadcastMessage("draw");
```

3   You're done! Save and test the movie to see how everything works. You should be able to use the arrow keys to move around within the scene. Try getting close to one of the objects in the scene. If it is one that has an info clip, you should see it appear when you approach. If the object links to another scene, getting close to the object should cause the background and objects to change.

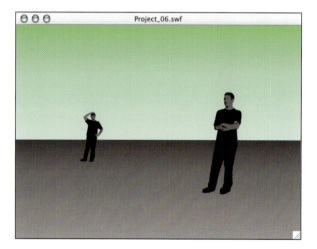

Note: If you like, you can compare your project to one included on the CD. The final project file, **Project_06.swf**, is located in the **Project_06** folder.

Now Try This

This project covered how to create a 3D environment from custom 3D classes, scripts, and mathematics that you can use to make immersive websites and games. You learned how to write class files, extend classes, import packages, use Quaternions and add key commands to control the scene.

Here are some ideas on how to apply the skills you've learned or use the project you've completed in other ways:

- You can create 3D mazes by linking multiple scenes that eventually lead to a final scene when the correct sequence is followed.

- You can create first-person shooter games and 3D chat-rooms from this code with additions that connect the objects in the scene to other users who are viewing the website.

- You can create galleries for your photos or artwork that users can navigate in 3D by substituting your images for those included here.

Adding Video to Create an Interactive Filmstrip

Andreas Heim works on cutting-edge digital media projects, including bringing Flash to devices, for Smashing Ideas in Seattle, Washington.

Andreas Heim
with contributions from Troy Parke

Several months ago, my friend Troy Parke approached me with this idea of placing a filmstrip to jazz up his personal website at http://www.troyparke.com, and asked me if I could do it. Sure thing, I said, and started working on it. It was easy for me to imagine how it would make the site more fun and engaging—and I hadn't seen such a thing before.

Shortly after adding the filmstrip to his site, a talent scout landed on it—and Troy got offered a rather nice new job.

It Works Like This

Anyone can do straight-up video, but this project explores adding video into an interactive filmstrip. Instead of just playing a video clip or having it wait until the user clicks a Play button, the clip is instead displayed as a sequence of images next to each other. As users roll over the individual images in the filmstrip, each of the images starts playing, creating rather interesting effects. Here are the basic steps of the project:

1 Place the FilmStrip component on the Stage and size it to your needs.

2 Import your own video clips for use inside the component.

3 Customize the look of the component by modifying the component parameters.

4 Dynamically size the component with the help of a listener so that the component is always as big as the Stage.

5 Add navigation options to the filmstrip by defining event handler functions and listening to the component of choice with addEventListener.

 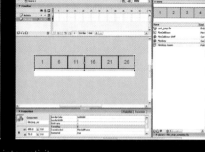

Make your filmstrip engaging by adding interactivity.

Set up the individual frames to play movies.

Preparing to Work

To prepare for this project, you will need to do the following:

1   Copy the **Projects/07/07 Film Strip Component** folder to your hard drive.

2   Open **film_strip_complete.fla** and click through the project so you can get familiar with what you'll be building. Close the file when you're finished.

Setting Up the Flash Movie

You will be building this project almost from scratch. The most important asset is the FilmStrip component, which is already placed in the Library.

1   Open the **film_strip_start.fla** file from the project folder you copied to your hard drive during "Preparing to Work."

2   Select the Film Strip layer. Open the Library and drag the FilmStrip component onto the Stage. Give it an instance name of filmStrip_mc. Because you will later use some ActionScript with the component, it is important to give it that instance name.

3   Set the X and Y coordinates of the component to 0. Using the Free Transform tool, extend the width of the component to the width of the Stage. Notice how the component changes as you scale it.

4   Save your work.

Adding Your Own Video Clip

You now have a filmstrip on the Stage, but it only shows some generic numbers. It's time to make it more interesting by adding your own video clip.

1   Create a new movie clip symbol by choosing Insert > New Symbol. Name the symbol FilmCellSnow. Also, make sure the Export for ActionScript and Export in First Frame options are selected and that the Identifier is also FilmCellSnow. If you don't see those properties in the dialog box, click the Advanced button.

2   Click OK to open the symbol for editing. Choose File > Import > Import to Stage. The Import dialog box should display the same folder containing the **film_strip_start.fla**. Otherwise, navigate to that folder. Select **cork_jump.flv** and click Open.

Note: The video clip used here was created using Sorenson Squeeze; the original source was a DV camera. Flash MX Professional 2004 has many more exciting ways of creating videos in FLV format. For more information, see Project 9, "Extending Video in Flash."

3   In the dialog box that opens, choose Yes to extend the Timeline to match the video.

4   The video clip is now in your symbol, but it's centered on the Stage. Position it at 0 for X and Y.

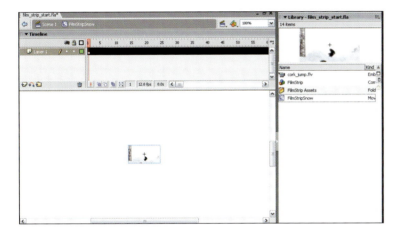

5   Right-click/Option-click on the FilmCellSnow in the Library. Select Convert to Compiled Clip.

This conversion precompiles the clip into SWF format so that this is the only time Flash needs to export this particular symbol. Whenever you do a test movie or publish later, the precompiled clip is grabbed and the export is much faster.

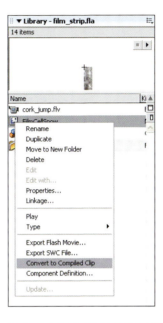

Note: When you publish your movie later, Flash doesn't need to export such a compiled clip again. However, for that to happen, you need to either delete the original symbol or make sure it doesn't export any more. If you delete the original symbol, it becomes impossible to edit it any more, so it's best to keep a backup of the original symbol in another FLA. Converting symbols this way can save you a lot of time when republishing. It also helps you protect symbols from editing.

As you might have noticed, you cannot edit the FilmStrip component; it is a compiled clip.

6. For some reason, Flash exports the video twice-once for the original FilmCellSnow symbol, and once for the compiled symbol named FilmCellSnow SWF. Instead of deleting the original symbol, right-click/Option-click the original FilmCellSnow symbol, select Linkage, and uncheck Export in First Frame.

7   Navigate back to the main Timeline and select the FilmStrip compo-
    nent on the Stage. In the Property inspector, find the videoSymbol
    property in the component parameters; you might have to scroll
    down. Change its value to FilmCellSnow and press Enter/Return.

Note: Instead of changing the component parameter and creating a
new symbol for the video clip, you can also find and modify the existing
FilmCellVideo symbol in the Library. However, then you will be able to
use only one video, even if you have multiple FilmStrip components on
the Stage.

Unfortunately, the live preview of the component cannot access the
video clip symbol you just created because it compiled itself before-
hand. Therefore, the component will look as it does in the figure in
Step 5, with just a gray placeholder. If you don't believe the live preview is for real, do a test movie to see the result on export.

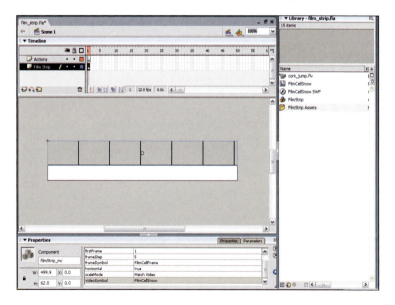

8   Save your work.

Customizing the Component Parameters

Now that you have taken care of changing the video symbol to your own
video clip, you can fine-tune the component by modifying its other component parameters. Although the specific settings used in this project are
included in the following steps, feel free to change the settings to match
your needs.

1   Set the borderColor to 0x000000. This sets the color of the frame
    around the video. The default is black.

2   Set the borderWidth to 2. This sets the width of the border frame
    around the video. If it's set to 0, no border is shown. The default is 1.

3   Set the firstFrame to 1. This defines the starting frame of the first cell
    in the filmstrip. The default is 1.

Note: Because the live preview doesn't show the new symbol, you
might want to change the videoSymbol back to FilmCellVideo when
experimenting with those.

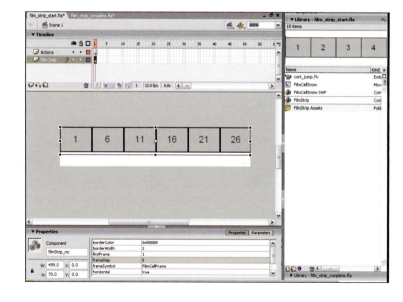

4 Set the `frameStep` to <u>5</u>. This defines how many frames will be stepped forward from cell to cell. The default is 1.

5 Set the `frameSymbol` to <u>FilmCellFrame</u>. This allows you to define your own symbol used for the frame around the video clip.

6 Set `horizontal` to <u>true</u>. This allows you to switch the filmstrip between a horizontal (default) and a vertical view.

> **Note:** Although the component flips its width and height, its bounding box does not. Therefore, the selection frame of the component remains unchanged until you manually change its size. This is an unfortunate limitation of the Flash authoring environment.

7 Set `scaleMode` to Match Video. This option allows you to modify how the video is rendered. Match Video shows the video at 100 percent. All other options could mean that the video becomes distorted. The default is Match Video.

> **Note:** The options other than Match Video are similar to the ones you have for the Stage in Flash:
>
> **No Scale**—Video is not scaled; it's centered in the frame and cropped if necessary.
>
> **Scale to Fit**—Video is scaled proportionally until it reaches the frame, either in x or y direction. It has no cropping, but a border might show.
>
> **Exact Fit**—Video is scaled in x and y direction to fit exactly into the border. Distortion might occur.
>
> **No Border**—Video is scaled proportionally until no border is visible. Cropping might occur.

8 Set `videoSymbol` to <u>FilmCellSnow</u>. This defines the symbol ID used for the video clip in the component.

9 Save your work.

Dynamically Sizing the Component

So far you have placed the FilmStrip component on the Stage and customized it to your needs. When you first placed the component on the Stage, you noticed that it is smart to show additional film cells if you give it more space. However, when you export the movie, it stays at that size, no matter how big your movie is. This can be fixed with a few lines of ActionScript.

1 Make sure you are on the main Timeline, select the Actions layer, and open the ActionScript editor if it's not already open.

2 You need to make sure the Stage is aligned properly and doesn't scale, so enter the following code:

Listing 7.1

```
Stage.scaleMode = "noScale";
Stage.align = "TL";
```

> **Note:** As opposed to previous versions of Flash, Flash MX 2004 is case-sensitive. Not only will the color-coding not work if you don't match identifiers exactly, but your code won't work either, and you might even get error messages when you export. For Flash, `Filmstrip` is now different from `FilmStrip` or `filmstrip`, so be careful what you type. This makes ActionScript more standards compliant; it works more similarly to JavaScript.

3 You need to be notified whenever the Stage changes its size. For this to work, a listener needs to be defined. Add this code:

Listing 7.2

```
var stageListener = new Object();
stageListener.onResize = function() {
  filmStrip_mc.setSize( Stage.width, Stage.height );
}
```

Note the instance name `filmStrip_mc`. Make sure you gave the component this instance name in the Property inspector; otherwise, this code won't work.

> **Note:** What is a listener? A *listener* is an object that receives events from an event source, such as the Stage or Mouse. A component can also be an event source. Multiple listeners can be defined for a single event source. That means different objects in your project can react to these events independently.

4   Now you have the listener, but it's not listening yet. Add this code to activate it, and you'll be finished:

Listing 7.3

```
Stage.addListener( stageListener );
```

This line of code is the piece of magic that activates the listener—it tells the Stage to add the listener object to its list of event recipients. In a way, this is like subscribing to a newsletter.

5   Save your movie and test it. Instead of just doing a test movie, publish it, and then watch it in the Standalone player.

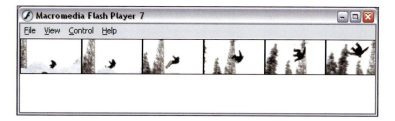

6   Resize the player and see the movie follow suit.

7   Roll over the individual cells to have them start playing.

8   Close the player.

Using the Component as Navigational Element

The main purpose of the FilmStrip component is to be a decorative element that invites visitors to interact with it. You might want to add additional functionality after the user clicks on the component, likely depending on which film cell the user actually clicked on. That is done relatively easily.

1   Add this code after the code in the Actions layer:

Listing 7.4

```
function handleEvent( event_obj ) {
  trace( "filmStrip_mc has been clicked: "
  ➥ + event_obj.target );
  trace( "and this cell: " + event_obj.value );
}
filmStrip_mc.addEventListener( "click", this );
```

The new way of receiving mouse and other events from components in Flash MX 2004 is by defining event handler functions and then listening to the component of choice using `addEventListener`. The above is an example of this. Because this is a simple component, it returns only `target` and `value` properties, as shown in the `trace` statements.

2 What to do with the event is up to you and the experience you want to create with your project. A simple example would be linking to different web pages by defining the following `handleEvent` function instead. Replace the code from Step 1 with this code:

Listing 7.5

```
var myLinks:Array = [
  "http://macromedia.com",
  "http://google.com",
  "http://yahoo.com",
  "http://cnn.com",
  "http://apple.com",
  "http://smashingideas.com"
];

function handleEvent( event_obj ) {
  var value = event_obj.value;
  var site = myLinks[ value ];
  if ( site != null && site != "" ) {
    getURL( site, "_blank" );
  }
}

filmStrip_mc.addEventListener( "click", this );
```

3 Save your work. Test the movie and click the Film Cells.

Now Try This

By now you've learned how to place the FilmStrip component on the Stage and size it to your needs, import your own video clips for use inside the component, customize the look of the component by modifying the component parameters, dynamically size the component with the help of a listener, and add navigation options to the filmstrip by defining event handler functions and listening to the component of choice with `addEventListener`.

> **Note:** The FilmStrip component is built on top of the new V2 architecture, on which all the new Macromedia UI components are built. You can find the source code for those on Windows in C:\Documents and Settings\<*user name*>\Application Data\Macromedia\Flash 2004\ en\Configuration\Classes\mx and a similarly named folder on the Mac.

Here is an idea on how to apply the skills you've learned or use the project you've completed in another way:

- Add a more custom border, make it look like actual film, or use more than one video clip. To do that, you will have to extend the component. The source files for the component are also included in a separate **film_strip_source** folder:

  - **film_strip_source.fla**—The source FLA of the component

  - **FilmStrip.as**—The class file for the FilmStrip component

  - **FilmCell.as**—The class file for the FilmCell component. The FilmCell component is a nested component of the FilmStrip component, making up an individual film cell.

> **Note:** These components were built using Flash MX 2004 Professional, for use with both versions of Flash MX 2004. The Pro version allows you to edit the class files directly in Flash, which is a great workflow improvement. If you own the regular version of Flash MX 2004, you can still edit the class files, but you will have to use an external text editor.

Controlling Your Text with CSS

Michelangelo Capraro
Duncan McAlester

Michelangelo Capraro   Duncan McAlester

Michelangelo Capraro is a multimedia designer and Co-Founder of Number 9, A Creative Digital Studio. He is a teacher and speaker on the topic of multimedia programming, design, and usability.

Duncan McAlester is a freelance designer/developer working in Southern California. He teaches at the University of California, Irvine Extension and the Laguna College of Art Design.

One thing that we find ourselves doing a lot these days is creating Flash content that is dynamic. The data may not actually exist in the Flash movie and might be pulled from a server or other source. One area that has always been sticky to deal with is the formatting of dynamic text in Flash. You used to always need to jump through ActionScript hoops to get it to look right, and when working on part-HTML, part-Flash websites—which seems to be much more common lately—we'd wish there was a way we could change the text in a Flash movie without touching the source code for it, the way you could in HTML by tweaking a CSS file. This usually involved a lot of XML and ActionScript and parsing. Wouldn't it be great if Flash allowed us to use existing CSS files to format the text in Flash?

Well, that's exactly what Flash MX 2004 does! This is really going to change the way we build our Flash movies and the way we build websites. With careful planning, you can build a web site that is part HTML and part Flash, and share the CSS files between them. Now our dynamic text fields can be as rich in formatting as our static text fields, helping us make the Flash movies even richer! And, those last-minute formatting changes can be tackled by tweaking a few lines of CSS—bam! The whole site can look different!

It Works Like This

You can tackle using CSS and HTML in Flash MX 2004 in a few different ways that this project will cover, starting with the easiest and ending with the more involved. In this project, you will create a painting browser that displays information about the paintings in text fields. Here are the basic steps of the project:

1   Build a simple painting browser that reads information about each painting, contained in a text file, and displays that information in a text field on the Stage.

2   The information for each painting will contain HTML tags for displaying an image and formatting the text using CSS.

3   Next you'll set up external CSS files to manage your code.

4   Load a separate CSS file that Flash will use to format your text.

 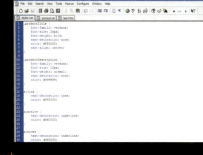

You'll combine the power of CSS with Flash.

New Product!

This **product** is one of the greatest products ever invented! After years of testing, the product is ready to release to the public. The product comes with a lifetime warranty too.

For a limited time, this product will be available for a special low price of $29.99! Thats a full 23off the recommended retail price of this fine luxury item.

Buy one for your home, your office, even yor garage! Adults like it, kids like it, even your pets will enjoy this amazing peice of high-quality furniture. Don't pass up this amazing offer and then regret it for the rest of your life. Each one of these beautiful, hand-crafted items is individually tested for reliability and strength. Under normal, everyday usage, we found these pieces to last an amazing 3 months! Thats weeks longer than any of the competitive brands out there.

This painting browser takes advantage of CSS to dynamically load

Preparing to Work

To prepare for this project, you will need to do the following:

1   Copy the **Projects/08** folder to your hard drive.

2   Locate the **Drawers.jpg** image and copy it file to the folder in which you will be saving your files on your hard drive.

3   Open a text editor such as TextPad, which is used in this project, or an HTML editor such as Dreamweaver.

Creating a Simple Style Sheet

In this first section, you will be creating a simple style sheet using Flash ActionScript and apply that style sheet to a text field on the Stage.

1   Create a new Flash document. You can use the default settings for the Stage size (550 × 400), the Background (#FFFFFF), and the Frame rate (12). Name the only layer in the Timeline field.

2   Choose the Text tool from the Tools palette and make a text field on the Stage. Select the new text field and make it dynamic by selecting Dynamic Text from the Text Type drop-down list in the Properties panel.

This allows ActionScript to control the properties of the text field.

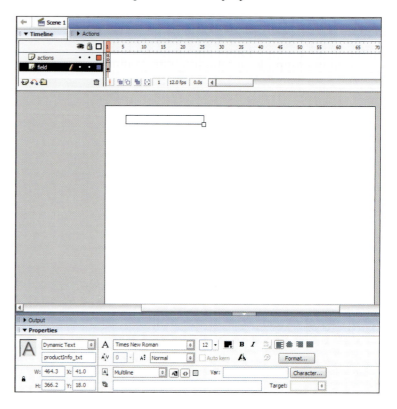

3   Set the line type of the field to Multiline and turn on the Render Text as HTML option for the field. These options allow you to put text containing HTML tags into your field and have Flash interpret those tags properly.

4   Give the field the instance name of productInfo_txt.

This allows ActionScript to access the field by name.

5 Stretch the field so that it takes up a good portion of the Stage.

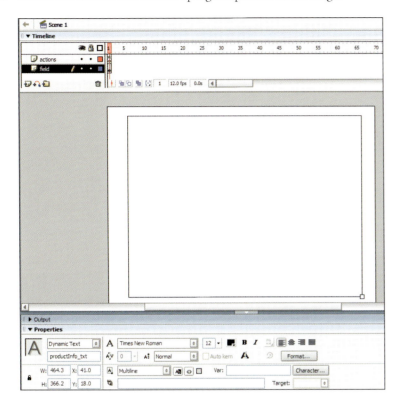

6 Create a new layer and name that layer <u>actions</u>. This is where you place the ActionScript code that controls the Text Field you created in the preceding steps.

7 Select the first frame in the actions layer and open the Actions panel.

Note: Turn line numbers on for the Actions panel by selecting View Line Numbers from the Actions panel menu in the upper-right corner of the Actions panel window. This makes it easier to follow along with the project.

In the bottom-left of your Actions panel, you should see a small tab with `actions:1` on it. This is a helpful indicator that tells you that you have the first frame of the actions layer selected. This comes in handy when you have larger projects with masses of code and clips.

8 Enter this code into your Actions panel:

Listing 8.1

```
productInfo_txt.htmlText = '<p>New Product!</p>';
```

This code sets the `htmlText` property of the field you created previously to whatever you assign it to after the equals sign. The `htmlText` property tells Flash to interpret the HTML tags rather than print the greater than and less than signs as regular text.

9 Test your movie by pressing Ctrl+Enter on Windows or Cmd+Return on the Mac. Your test movie should be displaying `New Product` on the screen.

10 Save this file in your Project folder (08) as <u>project8.fla</u>.

The Simple CSS Approach

Now that you have the basics down for getting text into the field with ActionScript, it's time to start formatting the text using CSS. Here you will create a simple style sheet using Flash ActionScript and apply that style sheet to the text field you created earlier.

1   Open the ActionScript panel for Frame 1 of the actions layer. Before the code you entered previously that populates the text field, enter this code to create your CSS object:

Listing 8.2

```
var product_ss = new TextField.StyleSheet();
product_ss.parseCSS("p { font-family: verdana; font-size:
➡ 24px; font-weight: bold; color: #ff0000; }");
productInfo_txt.styleSheet = product_ss;
```

2   Test your movie. You will notice that the text you saw before is now larger, red, and rendered using the Verdana typeface.

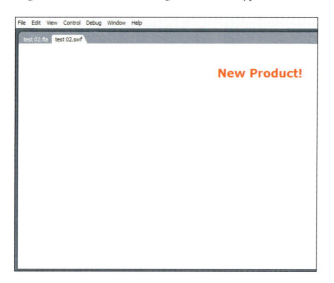

Now it's time to go through the ActionScript you added in Step 1 and see what each line does.

3   In this line of ActionScript, you create a new style sheet object, product_ss, using the style sheet class. You can think of a class as sort of a code template. The new operator creates an object from a class—in this case, the style sheet class—and assigns it to your product_ss variable. The style sheet object offers functions and properties for dealing with a style sheet that you might want to apply to a text field on the Stage.

```
var product_ss = new TextField.StyleSheet();
```

4   The parseCSS() function of a style sheet object takes any CSS code that you place in quotes between the parentheses and parses it into information that the product_ss object can later apply to a text field.

```
product_ss.parseCSS("p { font-family: verdana; font-size:
➡ 24px; font-weight: bold; color: #ff0000; }");
```

Note: Keep in mind that Flash supports only a selected set of CSS properties. Therefore, the CSS that works great in your browser might not have an effect on your text field in Flash. Here is a list of the supported CSS properties:

display	font-family	font-size
font-weight	text-decoration	color
text-align	text-indent	text-style
margin-left	margin-right	

Any other properties that might be defined in your CSS will be ignored.

Now you can quickly break down the CSS that you are passing to the parseCSS function.

This first element in the CSS (p { }) is describing style properties for the paragraph, or <p> tag. Individual style properties, such as font size and the typeface to use, are defined inside the curly brackets.

Here, with font-family: verdana;, you can choose to use the Verdana typeface for this style. The font-size property (font-size: 24px;) of the style sheet is pretty straightforward. You can use the font-weight property (`font-weight: bold;`) to control whether the type will be bold onscreen or the normal weight.

One thing to keep in mind is that although CSS allows you to specify text size using points (pt), pixels (px), or percentages (%), Flash interprets all of these as pixels.

In the last part of the CSS (`color: #ff0000;`), you define the color of the text. In this case, red was chosen.

This line of ActionScript sets the style sheet of the `productInfo_txt` text field to the styles defined in your `product_ss` object.

```
productInfo_txt.styleSheet = product_ss;
```

5 Save your work.

Using CSS Classes to Style Flash Text

So far, you have been able to style the text of the `<p>` tag. What if your text field has several paragraphs that you want to style differently? Next you'll see how this can be done.

Tip: Some of the lines of code you are writing are long, and you might be forced to scroll horizontally to see it all. One of the new features of the Actions panel in Flash MX 2004 is the ability to wrap long lines of text. You can turn on the Word Wrap feature by selecting it from the Actions panel menu, in the upper-right corner of the panel window. If you have a hard time scrolling horizontally to see long lines of code, you can turn on the new Word Wrap feature.

If you are already familiar with CSS, then you are probably comfortable creating CSS styles using classes. CSS classes basically allow you to create styles that are not specific to a type of tag, such as the `<p>` tag used in this project; rather, you can attach these styles to individual `<p>` tags within a document or field.

1 To define your CSS classes, open your Actions panel for Frame 1 of the actions layer. Change the line of code where you are parsing the CSS, line 2, to read like this:

Listing 8.3

```
product_ss.parseCSS(".productTitle { font-family: verdana;
➥font-size: 24px; font-weight: bold; color: #ff0000; }
➥.productDescription { font-family: verdana; font-size:
➥12px; font-weight: normal; color: #999999; }");
```

There are now two class descriptions that you are passing to the `parseCSS` function. You'll notice that this code no longer specifically addresses the `<p>` tag, but has replaced the p with `.productTitle` and `.productDescription`. These are CSS classes that don't apply to a specific HTML tag, so you will have to change the HTML that populates the text field to HTML that uses these new classes.

2 Assign the CSS classes in your text field by replacing the line of code where you change the `htmlText` property of your text field to read like this:

Listing 8.4

```
productInfo_txt.htmlText =
➥'<p class="productTitle">New Product!</p>
➥<p class="productDescription">
➥This <a href="#">product</a> is one of the greatest
➥products ever invented! After years of testing,
➥the product is ready to release to the public.
➥The product comes with a lifetime warranty too.</p>';
```

In the new HTML that you assigned to the text field's `htmlText` property, you have added a `class` attribute to each of the paragraph tags. The first paragraph is assigned the `productTitle` class, and the second paragraph is assigned the `productDescription` class.

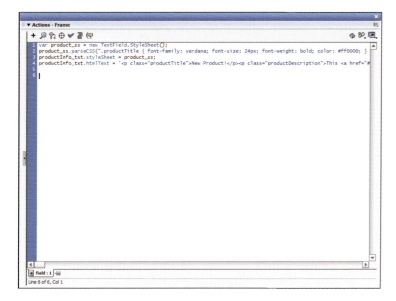

3   Test your movie. The text that you assigned to the `htmlText` property is displayed. The two paragraphs have distinctly different text styles.

4   Save your work.

Using External CSS Files

As you can see, CSS makes it easy to style text that you might be putting into a field dynamically; however, as you add more CSS classes to your style sheet object, you might find it slightly cumbersome to deal with the code by passing it directly to your `product_ss` style sheet object. In this part of the project, you will move your CSS code to an external CSS file, making it easier to manage.

The real power of CSS is realized when you use it from external CSS files. This makes it easy to use in multiple movies and even share with static HTML pages. For this next section, you will create a CSS file and write ActionScript that will load that file and apply the styles to the field you have on your Stage.

1   Open your favorite text editor and create a new file called styles.css. TextPad, a popular Windows text editor, is being used here. Dreamweaver is also a great tool for creating CSS files.

2   In your newly created CSS file, add these lines describing your classes:

Listing 8.5

```
.productTitle {
    font-family: verdana;
    font-size: 24px;
    font-weight: bold;
    text-decoration: none;
    color: #ff0000;
    text-align: center;
}

.productDescription {
    font-family: verdana;
    font-size: 12px;
    font-weight: normal;
    text-decoration: none;
    color: #999999;
}

a:link {
    text-decoration: none;
```

```
    color: #990000;
}

a:active {
    text-decoration: underline;
    color: #660000;
}

a:hover {
    text-decoration: underline;
    color: #ff0000;
}
```

Notice that a new property, text-align, has been added to the productTitle class and set to center. Also notice that three more classes have been added: a:link, a:active, and a:hover. These classes describe what a link should look like in a body of text (link), when the mouse cursor rolls over a link (hover), and when the mouse button is pressed on that link (active). In this case, the links are dark red. When the mouse is rolled over them, an underline should appear and the text should turn a brighter shade of red.

3 Now, back in your Flash movie, open the Actions panel for Frame 1 of the actions layer. You will be making some big changes, so go ahead and select all the ActionScript and delete it. Then add this code:

Listing 8.6

```
var product_ss = new TextField.StyleSheet();
product_ss.onLoad = function(success)
{
    if(success) {
        productInfo_txt.styleSheet = product_ss;
        productInfo_txt.htmlText = '<p
➥class="productTitle">
➥New Product!</p><p class="productDescription">
➥This <a href="#">product</a> is one of the
➥greatest products ever invented! After years of
➥testing, the product is ready to release to the
➥public. The product comes with a lifetime
➥warranty too.</p>';
    } else {
        trace("error getting CSS");
    }
}
product_ss.load("styles.css");
```

Before testing this new code, dissect it to see what will actually happen.

In the first line of ActionScript, you are creating a new style sheet object, as you did before.

In Line 2, you are assigning a function to the onLoad event of the product_ss style sheet object you created. Flash will call this function as soon as an external CSS file has finished loading into the product_ss object. On a slow web connection, for example, where things might take slightly longer to download, the code essentially waits for the CSS file to download before doing anything else. This ensures that you have style information loaded into your CSS object before trying to apply it to your text field.

When the `onLoad` event is called, Flash passes the `success` parameter to the attached function. This parameter is a Boolean value, which means it will be either `true` or `false` depending on whether the CSS file was loaded successfully. An example of the success parameter not being found would be if the CSS file were not found on the server.

After the CSS file has loaded successfully (Line 4), you assign the `product_ss` style sheet object to the text field on the Stage, the way you did in the previous exercises in this project.

In Line 6, you are assigning new text to the field on the Stage. Notice that the `<p>` tags now have class parameters. Also notice the link in the text (`<a href="#">`), which should display according to the `a:link`, `a:hover`, and `a:active` classes you defined in the CSS file earlier.

On Line 11 in the Actions panel, you load the CSS file after assigning the `onLoad` function. That way, you ensure that the CSS file doesn't load before the `onLoad` function is assigned and miss assigning the CSS object to the text field.

4   Test your movie. Try rolling over the word `product` in the second paragraph. Notice how it reacts when your mouse rolls over it and when you click on it.

Your CSS file is defining all of this. In fact, you can make changes to your CSS file and never have to make any changes to your movie because Flash loads and assigns the styles from your CSS file on-the-fly, at runtime. This can be a powerful tool when working on a Flash website and needing to make tweaks to text formatting; you can now do this without needing to open your original Flash FLA file.

5   Save your work. Congratulations! You have successfully moved your styles to an external CSS file.

The Real World: Loading Images from Image Tags

In this last part of the project, you will do the same with the actual content of the text field while discovering another of the cool new features of Flash MX 2004: loading images from image tags. In real-world projects, one use of the techniques you have learned so far in this project would be for styling data loaded from a server. An example of this might be loading individual product information from a catalog database. In this scenario, not only would your CSS styles be located in separate files, but the content for each product would not be in the Flash files, as you have been doing up until this point, but would be located in a database table.

For this final exercise, you will move the content of the text field to an external file and load it in much the same way that you have loaded the CSS file. This presents a much more realistic use of CSS for Flash projects. You will also be adding an image to the text field by inserting an image tag (`<img>`) into the HTML for the text field, demonstrating another new feature of Flash MX 2004.

1   Open your favorite text editor and create a new file called product.txt. This file will contain HTML that you'll load into Flash and display in the text field on the Stage.

2   When Flash loads a text file, it looks for variables and their values. Here, you will set up one variable called `productInfo`. Enter this on the first line of your new text file:

Listing 8.7

```
productInfo=
```

Now, you'll add the actual HTML that should be assigned to that variable. You'll build onto the HTML that you've been using in Frame 1 of the actions layer in your Flash movie by adding several more paragraphs of information. You'll want to have a lot of text for this particular exercise.

3   Enter this code after the equals sign in your product.txt file:

Listing 8.8

```
<p class="productTitle">Drawers Painting</p>

<p class="productDescription"><img src="Drawers.jpg"
➥align="right">This digital painting was painted in 2003
➥just before I moved to my new apartment in San Francisco.
➥The subject matter is a set of drawers that used to
➥reside in my living room.<br></p>
<p class="productDescription">This painting was created
➥using a PocketPC PDA with PocketArtist software by
➥<a href=http://www.conduits.com/target="_blank">
➥Conduits.com</a>.<br></p>
<p class="productDescription">This painting took a couple
➥of hours to do. It has a really nice, painterly quality
➥to it that I really like. Since there is no pressure
➥sensitivity on a PocketPC PDA, I rely on the opacity
➥option in the PocketArtist software to get different
➥color blends and the different brush sizes to get the
➥details I am looking for. When I was finally finished, I
➥transferred the painting to my desktop computer. I
➥noticed that the painting looked much more green in color
➥than it did on the PDA screen, which is slightly
➥washed-out.<br></p>
```

Notice when looking over the HTML text that an `<img>` tag loads an image called **Drawers.jpg**. You can find this image on the CD that came with this book, or you can use your own image. You should place this image in the same directory as your text file and Flash movie.

Note: When you're loading images using HTML or ActionScript, Flash only likes to load JPEG images. GIFs, PNGs, or any other popular web image formats work fine when imported into a Flash movie when you are authoring, but you won't see anything when attempting to load these with ActionScript.

4   In the Flash movie you've been using, open the Actions panel for the first frame of the actions layer. To load the text file, enter this ActionScript before the existing ActionScript:

Listing 8.9

```
var product_lv = new LoadVars();
product_lv.onLoad = function(success)
{
    if (success) {
        productInfo_txt.htmlText = product_lv.productInfo;

    } else {
        trace("error getting HTML");
    }
}
```

On the first line of the code you just added, you are creating a `LoadVars` object called `product_lv`. This object loads text files or server requests and reads the data looking for variables. After the text file or server data is loaded, it executes an `onLoad` event. It works very much like the style sheet object you created earlier.

Just as you did for the style sheet object, you'll want to define the function that is called when the `onLoad` event is executed before you actually load the text file. On Line 4, you test to see if loading was successful. If it was, you set the `htmlText` property of the text field on the Stage to the `productInfo` variable (which you defined in the product.txt file earlier) that is attached to the `product_lv` `LoadVars` object.

5 Now that the `onLoad` function for the `product_lv` object is defined, load the actual product.txt file. This will happen in the `onLoad` function for the style sheet object.

On Line 17 of your ActionScript for the actions layer, replace the line of code that sets the `htmlText` property of your `productInfo_txt` field on the Stage with this line of ActionScript:

Listing 8.10

```
product_lv.load("product.txt");
```

Although the code looks slightly complicated, the logic is fairly simple:

a   Create a new `LoadVars` object in which to load your text file.

b   Define the `onLoad` function that will be called when the product.txt file is fully loaded.

c   Create a new style sheet object to load the styles.css file.

d   Define the `onLoad` function for the style sheet object that is executed as soon as the styles.css file is finished loading. This, in turn, loads the product.txt file.

6   Test your movie. There should now be an image loading into your text field and text wrapping around the left side of the image.

Note: The Flash MX 2004 text field not only loads JPEG files using the <IMG> tag, but also loads other SWF files. This can be particularly useful if you need to display an interactive illustration of a product in a catalog.

7   Save your work.

Now Try This

By now you've learned how to build a simple painting browser that reads information about each painting and displays that information in a text field on the Stage, and load a separate CSS file that Flash will use to format your text.

Here are some ideas on how to apply the skills you've learned or use the project you've completed in other ways:

- Add more products to the product.txt file. On the CD in the **Projects/08** folder is an example of this project with multiple paintings being loaded from the same text file.

- Another change from loading the product.txt file is to load a URL that points to a server-side script, such as a PHP-based page. That PHP file can contain script to grab information from a database and return it to your LoadVars object.

- Use the same CSS file to format static HTML you might have on a site. This really maximizes the use of CSS on bigger projects that have both Flash and HTML content. The great part about using the external CSS file is that you can continue to change the style of the text without ever needing to re-export your SWF movie.

PROJECT 9 | Extending Video in Flash

James Williamson

James Williamson
is the Director of Training
at Lodestone Digital and has
more than nine years of
print design, web design,
and digital prepress
experience. He has been a
featured speaker at several
events, including DevCon,
MAX, and FlashForward.

To me, Flash is best at creating immersive interactive environments that expand and enhance traditional interfaces. With video support now two releases deep, I wanted to showcase the benefits (and risks) of adding video to projects. Unlike other application development tools for the web, Flash allows us to treat video as just another design element or object to add to the user experience. As developers, we sometimes become too focused on our technology of choice and forget our end users. Most of them don't care if we use the latest whiz-bang program or dated technology that's four years old; they just want to click on it and have it work. That's the beauty of Flash—with one fairly ubiquitous plug-in, you can offer an incredible range of interaction across multiple platforms.

In creating this project, I wanted to develop a simple, straightforward interface that integrates video into the experience. Far from being an experimental piece pushing the limits of the technology, my aim was to create a project that utilizes modular, generic code to create a complex series of interactions. As this project demonstrates, with properly planned video shoots and intelligent controls, video can be transformed from a passive, linear element to the dynamic focus of your projects.

It Works Like This

In this project you'll build a CD-based video catalog for a fictitious clothing company. You'll focus on some of the basic concepts of loading external video files and building complex interfaces to control the video in a nonlinear fashion. Here are the basic steps of the project:

1   Establish and load external variables to control the item price, description, and title of each item.

2   Load your FLV files into external SWF files and add frame labels to the timelines to allow playback control.

3   Add the necessary scripting to the individual video SWF files to enable the non-linear playback of the video.

4   Create additional variables to pass the identity of the selected video clip to the controllers.

5   Write generic scripts to control loading the appropriate video clips when requested and attaching the required playhead for each clip.

6   Add scripting to the individual playheads to control the video playback.

It's easy to enhance a site with video.

Users get instant interactivity as external movie clips work behind the scenes.

Preparing to Work

To prepare for this project, you will need to do the following:

1   Copy the **Projects/09/09 Extending Video** folder to your hard drive and open the file **Magnolia_final.swf** located in the **Finished Files** folder. To keep your file sizes down, the finished project includes video content for only the basic black dress.

2   Experiment with the video controls, accessory buttons, and menu options to get a feel for how the interactive catalog works.

Loading the Variable Object

Your first step will be to create a `Variable` object and load the necessary variables for each article of clothing. Doing so allows you to display the proper title, description, and price for each item selected. Although ideally this information would reside in a database, for this project, you will be loading variables from a text file.

1   Open the **clothing.txt** file in the Extending Video folder and examine the variables provided. Notice that titles, descriptions, and prices are included for only three items. Feel free to create more variables for the remaining items. Save and close the **clothing.txt** file.

```
clothing.txt - Notepad
File  Edit  Format  View  Help
&brezTitle=the breeze&
&brezDesc=Our most popular halter, this open cotton halter recalls the ocean
breeze and those cool summer nights. Available in Mango, Lime and Peach.&
&brezPrice=$50&
&basicTitle=basic black&
&basicDesc=Everyone needs a basic black! This dress allows you to always
arrive in style, whether you're dressing up or down. Shown with our elegant
Mahogany Jacket and Cabin Shirt. Available only in Black.&
&basicPrice=$299&
&siestaPrice=$190&
&siestaTitle=the siesta&
&siestaDesc=Perfect for a day at the beach or a night at the cabana, our
Siesta's floral print help bring the islands home! Available as shown.&
```

2   Open the **magnolia_start.fla** file and save it as my_magnolia.fla.

3   The first thing you'll do is load your external variables. Click on the first frame of the actions layer. Open the Actions panel and add this code:

Listing 9.1

```
//declare the Vars object and load the variables
clothingVars = new LoadVars();
clothingVars.load("clothing.txt");
```

This creates a new Vars object to hold your `clothing.txt` variables and then load the `clothing.txt` variables into the object.

Note: Using text files to store variables isn't as efficient as tying into a database. Sorting values is difficult, selecting subsets of data is almost impossible, and the entire text file must download before you access the variables. A text file is used in this project so that you can work locally.

4   Save and close the file.

Preparing External Video

Now that you have those variables out of the way, you can concentrate on your video files. Each item features four videos of your model showcasing the product. One video describes the item, another allows the user to examine the item in more detail, and two accessory items allow users to see the product with other outfits. Each of the clips also features your model reaching to press a corresponding accessory button to trigger the video, which creates a nice transition effect from one clip to another as users view the accessory items. Because your video controls use keyframe numbers, labels, and variables to control your video clips, you need to create SWF files that contain your FLV files and are structured according to your controller's needs. You'll tackle the description clip first.

1   Create a new file and name the file black_desc.fla. Change the movie size to 320×240 and change the frame rate to 30fps. Rename layer 1 as video and create two more layers: preloader and actions. Make sure that actions is the top layer.

2   Go to File > Import > Open External Library and open the **pre-loader.fla** file. Drag the preloader movie clip from the preloader Library into your black_desc Library. Close the preloader file.

Even though your project will load from a CD, it's always a good idea to put a preloader on any video content.

3   Drag an instance of the preloader movie clip to the Stage on Frame 1 and center it to the Stage, making sure that the preloader layer is your active layer. Add blank keyframes in Frame 2 of each layer.

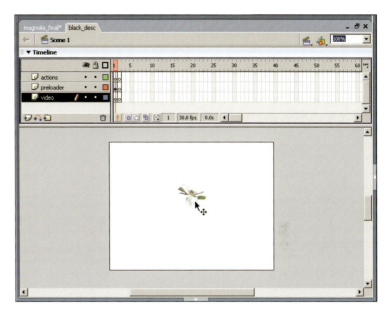

4   Select Frame 2 of the video layer. Choose File > Import > Import to Stage and select the **blackdress.flv** from the **Video** folder. A message appears notifying you that the selected video clip requires 502 frames to display properly. Click Yes to import the clip and expand your Timeline. Select the video clip on the stage and use the Property inspector to give it X and Y coordinates of 0 and 0. Insert a keyframe at Frame 503 of the actions layer and a holding frame at Frame 503 of the preloader layer. Save the file.

All the video files for your project are FLV files created using Sorenson's Squeeze software. FLV files are Flash's native video format and are typically used to stream video with the Flash Communication Server. These files also make great video files to embed into your projects because they have already been compressed and require no additional settings to import or export. Using the `NetStream` object, you can load FLV files externally without first embedding the video file. Although the video still loads progressively, this method simulates streaming video; therefore, it is unsuitable for your project.

5   Using the controller, preview the video file you've imported. (Don't worry that you can't hear the sound. That's not important right now.)

Notice that around Frame 331, something odd happens. Your model finishes talking about the item and moves to press an imaginary button. Later, at Frame 415, she changes again and presses a second, lower imaginary button. If this were to play back all at once, you wouldn't have much of an interactive catalog on your hands. Next, you'll modify your file to be controlled by your playhead.

6   Place a keyframe on Frame 330 of the actions layer. Add a stop action to the keyframe to stop your descriptive video after your model is finished talking. Place another keyframe on the actions layer on Frame 331. Using the Property inspector, label the frame acc1. Be careful to use this exact name; you'll be referencing that frame label later using your playhead.

Each video clip has two transition segments that simulate your model selecting an accessory item prior to that clip loading. You'll use the same frame labels (acc1 and acc2) to identify them in each video clip, which allows you to access the transitions with the same code for each clip.

Labeling frames allows you to mark a Timeline event for later reference in your code. Keyframes retain whatever frame label you have assigned them, even when they're moved. This, combined with the ability to use the same frame label name over multiple files, makes referencing frame labels more efficient than referencing frame numbers.

7   Repeat this process by placing a stop action on Frame 414 and labeling Frame 415 as acc2. Again, be careful to name the frame exactly. Add a stop action to the last frame of your movie to prevent it from looping back to the start.

Although you haven't seen it yet, your controller for the description clip will allow you to rewind, fast forward, play, and stop your video clip. As you can imagine, fast forwarding or playing past the final frame of the description would be disastrous. To prevent this, you'll create a variable that tells the controller which frame to stop at when playing or fast forwarding.

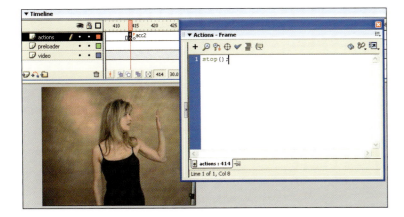

8 Select Frame 2 of the actions layer and open the Actions panel. In the Actions panel, type fwd_fr = 326;. This creates a variable named fwd_fr that will later pass the proper frame number to the controller. You'll learn later why Frame 326 was chosen.

Listing 9.2

```
fwd_fr = 326;
```

9 Adjust your publishing settings and publish your movie. Open the Publishing Settings dialog box and make sure the movie is only publishing the SWF file. Your description movie has sound, so you need to make sure you set your sound compression options. You set sound compression settings for embedded FLV files by using the Audio Stream settings. Set the sound compression settings to Speech and the sample rate to 22KHz. Click Publish to create your SWF file. Save and close the file.

Note: You don't have to use a third-party program like Sorenson Squeeze to create FLV files. Just right-click any embedded video file in your library, click Properties, and select the Export button to save your video file as an FLV file. The FLV file will employ the compression settings used to import the video file. Users of Flash MX 2004 Professional can take advantage of the FLV Export plug-in. Installing this plug-in will enable most industry-standard video-editing programs to export to the FLV format.

Preparing Nonlinear Video

In addition to watching a description of the selected item, your users will be able to "spin" your model around to view the outfit from front, side, and back views. Although your controller will do the real work behind this technique, setting up the external video file properly is crucial. This segment of the video features the model, Lisa, turning around in a tight circle. By clicking on right- or left-facing arrows, the video rewinds (turn left) or fast forwards (turn right). If you started in the first frame of the turn, your users wouldn't be able to turn left until they first turned right. You'll fix this by jumping to the middle of the turn and starting there. This will give the user the option to turn right or left from the beginning.

1   Create a new file named black_turn.fla. Set the movie size to 320×240 and the frame rate to 30fps. Rename layer 1 as video and create two more layers: preloader and actions. Make sure actions is the top layer.

2   Place the preloader symbol from the black_desc.fla in Frame 1 of the preloader layer.

3   Insert a blank keyframe in Frame 2 for all layers and a blank keyframe in Frame 3 for the actions and video layers.

Note: Video can certainly bring a tremendous amount of impact to any project, but you should include it only after careful consideration. Video can add a great deal of overhead to your Flash files and requires additional planning. Setting up video shoots can be a long and exhaustive process and can be wasted if the integration with the Flash movie isn't thought through prior to shooting. Having to reshoot scenes presents its own set of problems because video shot previously might not match the new scenes. To prevent this, make sure you script and storyboard your Flash files as much as possible prior to shooting video. Try to think of alternative scenes or additional content you might want. A good rule of thumb is to shoot more video and more takes than you think you'll need.

---

4   Select Frame 3 of the video layer. Choose File > Import > Import to Stage and select **blackdress_turn.flv** from the **Video** folder. Click Yes to extend the Timeline. Set the X and Y coordinates of the video clip to 0. Insert a keyframe for the actions layer and a holding frame for the preloader layer on the final frame.

Play through the video clip once and notice that the turn begins facing away from the camera and ends facing away from the camera. You'll jump to the middle of the turn and stop there.

5   Select Frame 133 of the actions layer. Label the frame middle and apply a stop action to the frame.

6   Select Frame 2 of the actions layer. Open the Actions panel and add the code in Listing 9.3. This code causes the video clip to jump to the middle of the turn and start there. You are replacing your fwd_fr variable with the number 242.

Listing 9.3

```
gotoAndStop("middle");
fwd_fr = 242;
```

7   Preview the video clip and note the frames where your accessory segments start. Using the same process employed in your black_desc.fla file, add the appropriate labels and stop actions for acc1 and acc2. Make sure to place a stop action prior to the start of an accessory clip and in the last frame.

8   Save and publish the file using the same publishing settings as before.

Note: Although you're using prebuilt FLV files for your video, Flash 2004's improved Video Import Wizard enables you to base compression quality settings on connection speed, edit your clips, and create a symbol on import that contains your video file.

Creating the Accessory Clips

Your last video clips feature Lisa modeling the current item along with a selected accessory. Although the clip is primarily linear in nature, users will still have the option of fast forwarding, rewinding, and stopping your clip. The accessory clips also contain the transition segments for each accessory. Setting up your accessory clips will be similar to your previous video clips.

1   Create a new file and name it black_asc1.fla. As before, set the movie size to 320×240 and change the frame rate to 30fps. Rename layer 1 as video and create two more layers: preloader and actions. Make sure actions is the top layer.

2   Place the preloader symbol from the black_desc.fla in Frame 1 of the preloader layer.

3   Create blank keyframes on Frame 2 of all layers. Choose File > Import > Import to Stage and select **blackasc1.flv** from the **Video** folder. Click Yes to extend the Timeline. Set the X and Y coordinates of the video clip to 0. Insert a keyframe for the actions layer and a holding frame for the preloader layer on the final frame.

4   As before, scrub the video clip by moving the playhead and note the frames where your accessory segments start. Using the previous steps, add the appropriate labels and stop actions for your transition segments using the acc1 and acc2 labels. Your first transition segment should start on Frame 293. Again, make sure to place a stop action prior to the start of an accessory clip as well as the last frame.

5   Select Frame 2 of the actions layer. Open the actions panel and add the following code to set the `fwd_fr` variable. Save and publish the file.

Listing 9.4

```
fwd_fr = 290;
```

6   Create a new file and save it as black_asc2.fla. Use the same document size and frame rate as the black_asc1.fla file. Use the previous method of creating a preloader for your file. As you work, make sure your layer structure matches the earlier file. Import blackasc2.flv and set the stop actions and acc1 and acc2 frame labels where needed. Set the fwd_fr variable to the frame number that is three frames before the end of the first segment (397). Save the file as black_asc2.fla and publish it.

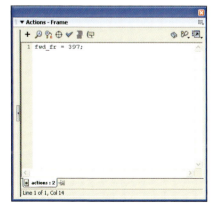

Note: After an FLV file has been embedded, you can replace it by right-clicking on the FLV file in the Library and choosing Properties. Just choose Import from the list of options and browse to find your new FLV file. Although the name of your FLV doesn't change in the Library, it uses the new FLV content. You can also quickly update your FLV files if you've modified them outside of Flash in the same manner.

Enabling Video Controls

Now that you've prepared your video files, you should take some time to review how the external files will be loaded and controlled. When an item is selected, the title, price, description, and a thumbnail of the article will appear. To avoid unwanted download time, you'll give the users the option to watch the video after they have selected an item by loading a preview file. The preview file and video content will load into a target movie clip named main_mc. When your video loads, you will also load an accessory file showing the accessory choices into a target movie clip named asc_mc. You want to make your code as generic as possible so that your preview file and controllers will work with all your video files. To do this, you'll create a variable that tells your controls which item is selected.

In the next segment, you'll modify your menu to activate the video preview file and load the item variable. You'll also examine your controllers and set their linkage properties to allow you to load them dynamically based on which video is selected.

1   Open your my_magnolia.fla file. Open the library and double-click the **menu** movie clip to enter Symbol Editing mode. Because you're working on the black dress video clips, you'll modify your code for the black button.

2   Select Frame 25 of the actions layer. You'll modify the existing code to create your item variable and then load your preview file. Change the existing code to add the following code in Listing 9.5. (New items are shown in bold.)

Listing 9.5

```
item = "black";
_parent.title_txt.text = _parent.clothingVars.basicTitle;
_parent.desc_txt.text = _parent.clothingVars.basicDesc;
_parent.price_txt.text = _parent.clothingVars.basicPrice;
loadMovie("images/basicb_still.jpg" , "_parent.still_mc");
loadMovie("preview.swf", _parent.main_mc);
```

Notice that the existing code uses the variables from the clothing.txt file that you loaded earlier. Take a moment to examine the dynamic text fields on the Stage to match the instance names with the variable content. When the black dress item is pressed, the title, price, description, and thumbnail will appear on the main Stage.

3.   Turn on your linkage for your two controllers so that you can call them dynamically depending on the video file loaded. In the Library, right-click on the asc_playhead movie clip and choose Linkage. Click the Export for ActionScript check box, accept the default identifier (asc_playhead), and check the Export in First Frame check box.

4   Repeat the procedure for the controller movie clip, giving it an identifier of playhead. Save the file.

Tip: By declaring an item variable each time the user selects an article, you can concatenate the variable into your `loadMovie` commands. Combined with calling your controllers dynamically, this technique allows you to write one set of generic code to control all clips.

Loading External Video

Now you're ready to load your video files. Your next task will be to add code to your preview file to load the video content and accessory file and attach your playhead controller. You will then return to your video files and add the code to activate your accessory transitions.

1   Open the file **preview.fla**. Click on Frame 1 of the actions layer and open the Actions panel. Add the following code:

Listing 9.6

```
//load the external video and attach the playhead controls

video_btn.onRelease = function() {
    _parent.main_mc.loadMovie (_parent.menu_mc.item +
    ➥"_desc.swf");
    _parent.asc_mc.loadMovie(_parent.menu_mc.item +
    ➥"_asc.swf");
    _root.attachMovie("playhead", "controller_mc", 10);
    _root.controller_mc._x = 185;
    _root.controller_mc._y = 243;

};
```

Your first two load movie commands concatenate the item variable and your naming convention (_desc for the description file, _asc for the accessory file, and _turn for the examination file) to load the proper video files. The attachMovie command attaches the playhead controls for the description video and positions it just below your video. Save and publish the file.

2   Open the black_asc.fla file and click on Frame 1 of the actions layer.

Instead of attaching a LoadMovie command to the appropriate item, you'll use the frame labels created earlier to trigger the transition segment for the current video clip.

3   In the Actions panel, add the following code. When complete, save and publish the file.

Listing 9.7

```
//launch the first accessory

acc1_btn.onPress = function() {
    _root.main_mc.gotoAndPlay("acc1");
}

//launch the second accessory

acc2_btn.onPress = function() {
    _root.main_mc.gotoAndPlay("acc2");
}
```

To finish your transitions, add code to your video clips that load the appropriate accessory video clips and attach the necessary controller.

4   Open the black_desc.fla file and move the playhead to Frame 414 (the last frame in your acc1 segment). Select Frame 414 of the actions layer and add the following code under the existing stop action:

Listing 9.8

```
//unload main controller and load accessory movie
_parent.controller_mc.removeMovieClip();
_parent.main_mc.loadMovie(_parent.menu_mc.item +
➥"_asc1.swf");
_root.attachMovie("asc_playhead", "asc_controller_mc",
➥10);
_root.asc_controller_mc._x = 82;
_root.asc_controller_mc._y = 243;
```

You use the removeMovieClip action to remove the existing controller and allow you to load your new controller.

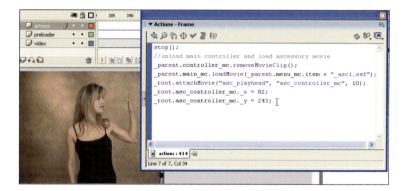

5   Repeat the process by adding the same code to Frame 503 (the last frame). Change the "_asc1.swf" in the loadMovie command to "_asc2.swf". This loads the second accessory movie. Save and publish the movie.

6   Open the **black_turn.fla**, **black_asc1.fla**, and the **black_asc2.fla** files and add the appropriate code to the end of each transition segment. Be sure to change the "_asc1.swf" to "_asc2.swf" on the second transition. Save and publish each file.

Tip: Although it's not always possible, when using video, you should try to match your Flash movie frame rate to your video frame rate (which is why your frame rates are at 30fps). Dropping frames from your video upon import can result in poor playback and loss of sync with imported audio.

Scripting Video Controls

Now that you have your video clips loading into your target movie clips, you can script your controls for your video. By embedding the video files into external SWF files and loading them into target movie clips, you can control your video by controlling your target movie clip. This is much more efficient than scripting controls for each video clip. Because you are giving your users multiple options when watching the video, you will also take advantage of conditional logic to manage playback depending on the current position in the Timeline. It is here that you will use the fwd_fr variable you created earlier.

1   Open the **my_magnolia.fla** file. Locate the **con_playhead** movie clip and double-click the symbol to enter Symbol Editing mode. Move the Timeline to examine the controller.

The first playhead controls the description clip, and the second controls the turn clip. The toggle button allows the user to switch back and forth between the two clips. Note the frame labels you will use to help you toggle your playheads.

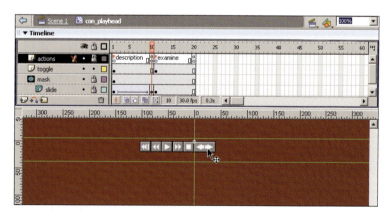

2   After you examine the con_playhead symbol, double-click the controller movie clip to edit the clip. Click on Frame 1 of the actions layer and open the Actions panel.

3 Begin by adding the code to control the toggle function:

Listing 9.9

```
//playhead toggle controls
controls_mc.toggle_btn.onPress = function() {
    if (controls_mc._currentframe == 10) {
        controls_mc.gotoAndPlay("examine");
        _parent.main_mc.loadMovie(_parent.menu_mc.item +
        ➥"_turn.swf");
    } else {
        controls_mc.gotoAndPlay("description");
        _parent.main_mc.loadMovie(_parent.menu_mc.item +
        ➥"_desc.swf");
    }
};
```

This code examines the playhead controls when the toggle button is pressed. Using the if statement, your toggle button checks the playhead's current state. If the current frame is Frame 10, your description movie controls, the playhead loads the **_turn** movie and jumps to the turn controls. If the current frame is not 10, which would mean the turn controls were active, the toggle control loads the **_desc** movie and turns to the description playhead controls. Note the use of the item variable to load the current movie.

4 Make writing your button controls a little easier by assigning path definitions. Beneath your current code, add the following:

Listing 9.10

```
//path definition to playhead controls
playheadPath = controls_mc.playhead_mc;
//path definition to examine controls
examinePath = controls_mc.examine_mc;
```

This allows you to save time when writing your playhead commands.

5 You will now begin assigning controls to your playhead, starting with your description clip controls. Add the code shown in Listing 9.11

Listing 9.11

```
//playhead controls

// reset movie controls
playheadPath.fullrew_btn.onPress = function() {
    _root.main_mc.gotoAndPlay(1);
};
// rewind movie controls
playheadPath.rew_btn.onPress = function() {
    _root.main_mc.onEnterFrame = function() {
        _root.main_mc.gotoAndStop(_root.main_mc._
        ➥currentframe-6);
    };
};
playheadPath.rew_btn.onRelease = function() {
    delete _root.main_mc.onEnterFrame;
};
// play movie controls
playheadPath.play_btn.onPress = function() {
    if (_root.main_mc._currentframe >=
        ➥_root.main_mc.fwd_fr){_root.main_mc.stop();
    }else {
    _root.main_mc.play();
    }
};
// fast forward movie controls
playheadPath.ffw_btn.onPress = function() {
    _root.main_mc.onEnterFrame = function() {
    if (_root.main_mc._currentframe >=
        ➥_root.main_mc.fwd_fr){
        ➥_root.main_mc.stop();
    }else {
        _root.main_mc.gotoAndStop(_root.main_mc._
        currentframe+3);
        }
    };
};
playheadPath.ffw_btn.onRelease = function() {
    delete _root.main_mc.onEnterFrame;
};
// stop movie controls
playheadPath.stop_btn.onPress = function() {
    _root.main_mc.stop();

};
```

For the rewind and fast forward controls, you will use an `onEnterFrame` event to keep the clip rewinding or fast forwarding while the button is held down. Notice that you are also deleting the `onEnterFrame` event after the button is released. If the `onEnterFrame` is not deleted after use, it continues to run. Not only can this hamper your functionality, but it can cause the Flash Player performance to suffer as well. You also need your playhead to be smart. If your descriptive segment has finished playing, the Play button must be disabled; otherwise, the video clip would continue playing into the accessory transition.

Likewise, the Fast Forward button must keep track of the clip's current position. The Fast Forward button must stop at the end of the descriptive segment and not continue into the transition segments. To do this, you'll use an `if` statement and the `fwd_fr` variable you created earlier to let you know where your descriptive segment boundaries are. Because your fast forward command will skip three frames at a time, set your `fwd_fr` variable to three frames before the last frame of your descriptive segment.

You might notice that the rewind frame subtraction is higher than the fast forward frame addition. Due to the way the Flash Player buffers content, it must load frames played backward completely again, slowing playback. By increasing the frame amount, you help your controls appear to play back at the same speed. You'll notice this difference more on slower systems.

6   Using the same logic for your turn controls, you will now add the code that allows users to "spin" the model to the left or right. After your description playhead controls, enter the code shown in Listing 9.12.

Listing 9.12

```
//turn controls

//left turn
examinePath.left_btn.onPress = function() {
    _root.main_mc.onEnterFrame = function() {
        _root.main_mc.gotoAndStop(_root.main_mc._
➥currentframe-5);
    };
};
examinePath.left_btn.onRelease = function() {
    delete _root.main_mc.onEnterFrame;
};
//right turn
examinePath.right_btn.onPress = function() {
    _root.main_mc.onEnterFrame = function() {
    if (_root.main_mc._currentframe >=
➥_root.main_mc.fwd_fr){
        _root.main_mc.stop();
    }else {
        _root.main_mc.gotoAndStop(
➥_root.main_mc._currentframe+2);
        }
    }
}
examinePath.right_btn.onRelease = function() {
    delete _root.main_mc.onEnterFrame;
};
```

Although your left turn doesn't require an `if` statement, your right turn, if unchecked, would continue into your accessory transition segments. You will also use an `onEnterFrame` event to allow for a continuous turn.

7 Double-click the asc_playhead movie clip to enter Symbol Editing mode. This playhead will control your accessory movie clips. As you might notice, it is almost identical to your main controller except for one difference. Instead of a toggle control, this playhead has a Reset button, which unloads the accessory movie and reloads the description clip.

8 Select Frame 1 of the actions layer. Add the following code for your playhead controls:

Listing 9.13

```
//playhead controls

// full rewind movie controls
fullrew_btn.onPress = function() {
    _root.main_mc.gotoAndPlay(1);
};
// rewind movie controls
rew_btn.onPress = function() {
    _root.main_mc.onEnterFrame = function() {
        _root.main_mc.gotoAndStop(_root.main_mc._
        ➥currentframe-6);
    };
};
rew_btn.onRelease = function() {
    delete _root.main_mc.onEnterFrame;
};
// play movie controls
play_btn.onPress = function() {
```

```
    if (_root.main_mc._currentframe >=
    ➥_root.main_mc.fwd_fr){
        _root.main_mc.stop();
    }else {
    _root.main_mc.play();
    }
};
// fast forward movie controls
ffw_btn.onPress = function() {
    _root.main_mc.onEnterFrame = function() {
        if (_root.main_mc._currentframe >=
        ➥_root.main_mc.fwd_fr){
        _root.main_mc.stop();
        }else {
            _root.main_mc.gotoAndStop(_root.main_mc._
            ➥currentframe+3);
        }
    };
};
ffw_btn.onRelease = function() {
    delete _root.main_mc.onEnterFrame;
};
// stop movie controls
stop_btn.onPress = function() {
    _root.main_mc.stop();
};
```

9 To finish your accessory playhead, you need to enable the Reset button to unload the current movie and replace it with the description movie, and unload the current controller and replace it with your main controller. Below your current code, add the following:

Listing 9.14

```
// reset movie controls

reset_btn.onPress = function() {
    _parent.main_mc.loadMovie (_parent.menu_mc.item +
    ➥"_desc.swf");
    _root.attachMovie("playhead", "controller_mc", 20);
    _root.controller_mc._x = 185;
    _root.controller_mc._y = 243;
    _parent.asc_controller_mc.removeMovieClip();

}
```

10 Finally, you need to modify your menu controls slightly. Currently, when a user clicks on the black dress menu item, the preview file is loaded. When multiple items are available, the user will select items after loading and viewing other items. If a video clip is active, you need to unload the playhead controls for the current clip and the current **_asc** SWF file. Double-click the menu movie clip to enter Symbol Editing mode. Select Frame 25 of the actions layer to move to the black dress button code. Add the following to the code to unload any playhead controls below the `item` variable:

Listing 9.15

```
_parent.asc_mc.unloadMovie();
_parent.controller_mc.removeMovieClip();
_parent.asc_controller_mc.removeMovieClip();
```

11 Save and test your file. The Black Dress item should load all variables and activate the video content. Test your playhead controls to verify the control over the video clips. Compare your finished file with the **magnolia_final** file in the **finished files** folder.

Note: You might have noticed that your controllers only need two pieces of information to work with any of your video clips, the frame number that marks the end of the current segment, and the item name of the current article. This makes your controllers excellent candidates for being components.

Now Try This

By now you've learned how to load your FLV files into external SWF files, and then load those files at runtime into a target movie clip to control the video with the wide array of methods available to the movie clip object. You've also learned how to modify the external SWFs and write scripts for controllers that allow you to choose when and where along the timeline a segment plays and set boundaries to control segment play.

Here are some ideas on how to apply the skills you've learned or use the project you've completed in other ways:

- To reinforce the concepts of the project, you can modify the .txt file to contain new variables, create new video SWF files, and modify the menu movie clip to load the new content. There are additional video files for two other items in your project folder.

- Create functions for various transitions and then select those transitions at random to switch between video clips. By using keyframe labels with multiple video clips, you can write generic code to move around the Timelines of your clips in any manner you want.

- Try building playheads and transitions based on mouse movement or other user interactions.

PROJECT 10

Creating an Information Display System

by Todd Marks

Todd Marks
is an avid developer,
designer, instructor, and
author of information
display technologies. He is
also a Macromedia Certified
Developer, Designer, and
Subject Matter Expert, and
currently works as a software
engineer for the Media
Edge division of
Exceptional Software.

During the course of several months, last fall I worked on developing a Flight Information Display System (FIDS) with Arinc Information Technology. This FIDS is unique to the market in the fact that the front end was developed using entirely ActionScript, and is comprised of 21 components. These components allow the FIDS to display everything from arrival and departure information, to video and virtual paging. The key thing, however, is that not only the content but also the appearance of the information is truly dynamic and depends entirely on the XML passed into the system.

My main developmental goal is to facilitate the creation of a hardware and software solution that allows information to travel infinite distance over zero time. This system would allow all knowledge to be disseminated and learned instantaneously, and have a delivery vehicle that is entirely autonomous. This project—creating an Information Display System that can display information (whose appearance in addition to data is governed entirely by XML)—is a big step in that direction.

It Works Like This

This simple information display system sews together a couple of new Macromedia components—the DataGrid and Loader—to make a light system that allows you to dynamically place information on the Stage at runtime. Here are the basic steps of the project:

1 Create the XML file and structure that allows you to pass styles and data into a display system.

2 Develop the simple information display system to deliver that content.

XML and DataGrid component.

System in Action.

Preparing to Work

To prepare for this project, you will need to do the following:

1 Copy the **Projects/10** folder to your hard drive.

Note: You can copy **background.swf** to add a nice border to your display, although it will be used simply to show how external media can be loaded into the system.

---

2 Take a look at the completed SWF file **infoDisplay_final.swf**. You will see a dataGrid with some sample content. All of the information displayed on screen was passed in as either XML attributes, text, or as separate media files.

Designing the XML Container File

The first thing you need to do is create an XML file that can hold all your style attributes and data. The XML file—and more specifically the data being transferred—is a key ingredient in the architecture of an information display system. In this case, you are going to pass information to the new DataGrid and Loader components, so ideally, you want to build in as many "attributes" of those components into your XML file as possible.

Note: An *XML schema* is a guide that details what you can and cannot have in your XML file, as well as the way in which you must organize it so that the display system reads it correctly.

Flash is great at reading XML because it can read all the attributes on an XML node with a single method and make them available as an array. Therefore, for every property that is supported by the DataGrid and other components in your information system, you will add attributes to your XML schema.

1 Open any XML or text editor and save it as data.xml.

2 Add this initial tag to the XML document:

Listing 10.1

```
<display>
```

3 Add this tag on the next line of the text document to hold the information for your background SWF file:

Listing 10.2

```
<media X="0" Y="0">background.swf</media>
```

Flash can import not just SWF files but JPGs and MP3s (since Flash MX)—and now with Flash MX 2004, FLVs. For now, you are simply going to add an SWF to the Stage, but you'll try using all the different file types that are possible.

Note: This simple information display system can load a host of different media types. You load these media types by including them in the XML document.

---

4 Add this code:

Listing 10.3

```
<grid X="25" Y="26" Width="750" Height="260"
➥headerColor="501000" spaceColEvenly="true"
➥headerHeight="40" rowHeight="20" backgroundColor=
➥"700000" borderColor="000000">
```

The `<grid>` tag holds the most attributes in your XML document. Each change in the value of an attribute in this tag affects the appearance of the grid that holds the data.

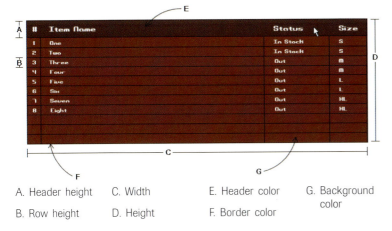

A. Header height
B. Row height
C. Width
D. Height
E. Header color
F. Border color
G. Background color

5 Add the data to the grid. You will do so within `<Row>` and `<Column>` tags. Add the following tags in the XML document:

Listing 10.4

```
<row>
    <column Name="Size">S</column>
    <column Name="Status">In Stock</column>
    <column Name="Item_Name">One</column>
    <column Name="Num">1</column>
</row>
<row>
    <column Name="Num">2</column>
    <column Name="Item_Name">Two</column>
    <column Name="Status">In Stock</column>
    <column Name="Size">S</column>
</row>
<row>
    <column Name="Num">3</column>
    <column Name="Item_Name">Three</column>
    <column Name="Status">Out</column>
    <column Name="Size">M</column>
</row>
<row>
```

```
    <column Name="Num">4</column>
    <column Name="Item_Name">Four</column>
    <column Name="Status">Out</column>
    <column Name="Size">M</column>
</row>
<row>
    <column Name="Num">5</column>
    <column Name="Item_Name">Five</column>
    <column Name="Status">Out</column>
    <column Name="Size">L</column>
</row>
<row>
    <column Name="Num">6</column>
    <column Name="Item_Name">Six</column>
    <column Name="Status">Out</column>
    <column Name="Size">L</column>
</row>
<row>
    <column Name="Num">7</column>
    <column Name="Item_Name">Seven</column>
    <column Name="Status">Out</column>
    <column Name="Size">XL</column>
</row>
<row>
    <column Name="Num">8</column>
    <column Name="Item_Name">Eight</column>
    <column Name="Status">Out</column>
    <column Name="Size">XL</column>
</row>
```

6 Add the final tags to the document:

Listing 10.5

```
</grid>
</display>
```

7 Save the file as data.xml in the same directory as the Flash file you are about to create.

Preparing the Flash Movie

Now that you've created your data document, it's time to open a new movie and add some components to its Library.

Note: The DataGrid component that you'll be using is only included in the components Library with Flash MX 2004 Professional. You can, however, also find the DataGrid component for nonprofessional users in the ComponentFLA folder in the Flash MX 2004 directory (**\Flash MX 2004\en\First Run\ComponentFLA\StandardComponents.fla**).

1   Open a new Flash document. Make its dimensions 800×600, change the background to #700000, and set it to 21 frames per second. Also, go ahead and save the file as infoDisplay.fla.

Note: Keep in mind that the frame rate of this movie will dictate the frame rate at which all other externally loaded SWF files play as well.

---

2   Open the components project and drag and drop an instance of the DataGrid and Loader components from the UI Components folder.

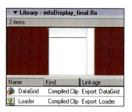

3   Delete the components from the Stage. Don't worry—the components have already been added to the Library where you need them. (Unfortunately, you cannot drop components directly into the Library.)

Sewing Together the Components

It will be a long time before code is entirely omniscient, so for now, you are going to have to write a few functions to get these components working as part of the same system.

1   Click on the first frame and open the Actions panel (F9).

2   Start by declaring some initial variables:

Listing 10.6

```
_global.totalXMLFiles=0;
_global.totalMedia = 0;
_global.totalGrids = 0;
_global.totalAssets = 0;
```

These four variables are fairly self-explanatory, but because you can use this system to display multiple media files, multiple grids, and so on, you'll want to keep track of the total number of these assets.

Note: You can make the code in Step 3 into its own component such that the only line you'll ever need to change would be the location of the XML to load. For now, keep the code on the main Timeline.

---

3 Add a function to open an external asset, such as an SWF file, using the new Macromedia Loader component:

Listing 10.7

```
function loadMedia(_oAttributesArray, _data) {
    //This function adds an SWF or JPG file to the Stage
    _root.attachMovie("loader", "oLoader"+(++_global.
➥totalMedia),++_global.totalAssets);
    _root["oLoader"+_global.totalMedia]._x =
➥ _oAttributesArray["X"];
    _root["oLoader"+_global.totalMedia]._y =
➥ _oAttributesArray["Y"];
    _root["oLoader"+_global.totalMedia].scaleContent =
➥false;
    _root["oLoader"+_global.totalMedia].contentPath =
➥ _data;
    _root["oLoader"+_global.totalMedia].load();
}
```

The parameters that are passed into this function are the `Attributes` array, which holds the information about the `<media>` that is going to be loaded, as well as the URL of that media.

You can add any component to the Timeline from the Library by using the `attachMovie` method.

As the second parameter of the `attachMovie` method, we set the name of the attached object to `"oLoader"+(++_global.totalMedia)`. By having a concatenated name we can increment the value of the variable `_global.totalMedia` so that every time this function is called a new instance of the loader component is used. Having `++` preceding this variable will increment the variable every time it is called.

After attaching the new loader MovieClip to the timeline, we set its x and y positions by setting those properties equal to their passed in values found in the Attributes array. We then set the `scaleContent` property to `false`, set the `contentPath` equal to the `_data` parameter, which is also passed in to the function, and then load the content.

4 To add the `CreateGrid` function, add this code after `loadMedia`:

Listing 10.8

```
function CreateGrid(_oAttributesArray) {
    //This function adds an information grid to the Stage
    _global.iRow=0;
    ++_global.totalGrids;
    _root.attachMovie("DataGrid",
➥"oGrid"+_global.totalGrids,++_global.totalAssets);

_root["oGrid"+_global.totalGrids].setSize(Number(_oAttributes
➥Array["Width"]), Number(_oAttributesArray["Height"]));
    _root["oGrid"+_global.totalGrids]._x =
➥ _oAttributesArray["X"];
    _root["oGrid"+_global.totalGrids]._y =
➥ _oAttributesArray["Y"];
    //this["oGrid"+_global.totalGrids].alternatingRowColors
➥(0x700000,0x000000);
    if (_oAttributesArray["spaceColEvenly"] eq "true") {
        _root["oGrid"+_global.totalGrids].spaceColumns
➥Equally();
    }
    _root["oGrid"+_global.totalGrids].setStyle
➥("vGridLineColor",
➥"0x"+_oAttributesArray["borderColor"]);
    _root["oGrid"+_global.totalGrids].setStyle
➥("hGridLineColor",
➥"0x"+_oAttributesArray["borderColor"]);
    _root["oGrid"+_global.totalGrids].setStyle
➥("headerColor",
➥"0x"+_oAttributesArray["headerColor"]);
    _root["oGrid"+_global.totalGrids].headerHeight = 30;
    _root["oGrid"+_global.totalGrids].rowHeight = 20;
    _root["oGrid"+_global.totalGrids].borderColor =
➥"0x"+_oAttributesArray["borderColor"];
    _root["oGrid"+_global.totalGrids].backgroundColor
➥="0x"+ _oAttributesArray["backgroundColor"];}
```

If you read through the code in this function, you probably noticed that the first major thing to do is attach an instance of the Grid component from the Library with the line of code:

```
root.attachMovie("DataGrid", "oGrid"+_global.totalGrids,
++_global.totalAssets);
```

Then you assign style values to the Grid component by setting its properties equal to the values of the attributes that were loaded from the data.xml file.

The new instance of the grid is called `"oGrid"+_global.totalGrids` so that you can have multiple grids on one page with unique names and unique levels. By concatenating a variable to the end of a string to name an instance of an object, you can increment that variable and create multiple unique grids.

Note: The `CreateGrid` function is little more than a place to set the individual properties of the Grid component. For instance, the line

```
root["oGrid"+_global.totalGrids].setStyle("headerColor",
➥"0x"+
    oAttributesArray["headerColor"]);
```

sets the `headerColor` of the new grid instance equal to the value that was initially passed in from the XML file. Note that several other style properties, such as text font and text color, have not been implemented.

---

5   Add the `AddRow` and `AddColumn` functions.

Listing 10.9

```
function AddRow() {
    _global["arrRow"+(++_global.iRow)] = new Array();
}

function AddColumn(_oAttributesArray, _data) {
    _global["arrRow"+_global.iRow][_oAttributesArray
➥["Name"]] = _data;
    _global["arrRow"+_global.iRow].reverse();
}
```

The Grid component allows its rows, cells, and appearance to change even after the initial creation of the component. When you're developing these functions, you can call them something like `AddNewRow`, but built-in methods of the Grid component are already available to utilize in your user-defined functions.

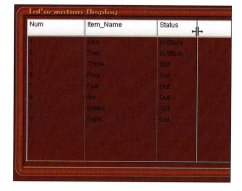

Note: When you set `resizableColumns` (which is a property of the new DataGrid component) to `false`, the user cannot resize the columns of the grid.

---

6 Add the Parse function.

Listing 10.10

```
function Parse(_firstchild) {
//Recursive function that parses XML
    if (_firstchild != null) {
        var sNode = _firstchild.nodeName;
        var oAttributesArray = _firstchild.attributes;
        switch (sNode) {
        case ("display") :

            break;
        case ("media") :
            this.loadMedia(oAttributesArray, _firstchild.
            ➥firstChild);
            break;
        case ("grid") :
            _global.totalRows=0;

            this.CreateGrid(oAttributesArray);
            break;
        case ("row") :
            this.AddRow();
            break;
        case ("column") :
            this.AddColumn(oAttributesArray, _firstchild.
            ➥firstChild, _firstchild.nextSibling);
            break;
        default :
            //unexpected tag encountered
            error = true;
            break;
        }
        var oNextChildXml = _firstchild.firstChild;
        while (oNextChildXml != null) {
            this.Parse(oNextChildXml);
            oNextChildXml = oNextChildXml.nextSibling;
        }
    }
}
```

The next function you need to add is the function that does most of the data organization. This function, called Parse, reads the XML file recursively and tries to call a function for every tag that it encounters. In this case, you are going to read the <display>, <media>, <grid>, <row>, and <column> tags. Then you'll send the attributes and data for those tags to the respective functions you created.

Note: Recursive means to "call oneself." In this case the function Parse calls itself within the function. In doing so the function can essentially walk through the nodes of the XML until it reaches the last child of each node. When a last child is reached it will then not call itself, and move to the next child of the parent node. When all nodes are read, the function call is complete, and all of the XML has been parsed.

7 Add a function to create an XML object inside of Flash and to load your data file. Add this code:

Listing 10.11

```
function loadXMLData(_sURL, _iFile) {
//This function creates an XML object and loads a file
➥into it
    this["oDataXml"+_iFile] = new XML();
    this["oDataXml"+_iFile].ignoreWhite = true;
    this["oDataXml"+_iFile].onLoad = function(_bSuccess) {
        if(_bSuccess) {
            Parse(this.firstChild);
            //populate final grid
            oData = new Array();
            for (var x=1; x<=_global.iRow; x++) {
                oData[x-1]=_global["arrRow"+(x)];
            }
            _root["oGrid"+_global.totalGrids].dataProvider
            ➥ = oData;
            oData = null;
        } else {
            error=true;
        }
    };
    this["oDataXml"+_iFile].sendAndLoad(_sURL,
    ➥this["oDataXml"+_iFile]);
}
```

Flash MX Professional 2004 users have several additional components over those of nonprofessional users. Many of these components are dedicated to sending and loading data. One of these is the XML connection component, which is similar to `loadXMLData` in functionality, except that it has several advanced features, such as concurrent data transfers.

8   Add a line to kick everything off and feed in your XML data. Add the following:

Listing 10.12

```
loadXMLData("data.xml", totalXMLFiles++);
```

9   Save and test your file. You should see a grid showing your data and attributes from the data.xml file. You should also be able to select the individual cells and resize each column. Note that the completed project is **infoDisplay_final.fla**, which you can find on the CD-ROM.

Now Try This

By now you've learned how to create the XML file and structure that allows you to pass styles and data into a display system, and develop the simple information display system to deliver that content.

Here are some ideas on how to apply the skills you've learned or use the project you've completed in other ways:

• Extend the system to fit your needs by adding several additional `<media>` and `<grid>` tags to the XML document, and explore the freedom to place a variety of media on the Stage.

• Continue to add attributes to the tags in the XML file and build functionality to receive those tags in the Flash file.

• Harness the power of Flash to create information display systems such that they can be delivered using a web browser, changes can be made remotely, and a page can change its appearance without having to refresh the entire page.

• Add a back end database and system to generate XML data based on particular queries against the database.

JSFL: Using Flash's New Automation Language to Create Text Effects

Michelangelo Capraro
Duncan McAlester

Michelangelo Capraro   Duncan McAlester

Michelangelo Capraro is a multimedia designer and Co-Founder of Number 9, A Creative Digital Studio. He is a teacher and speaker on the topic of multimedia programming, design, and usability.

Duncan McAlester is a freelance designer/developer working in Southern California. He teaches at the University of California, Irvine Extension and the Laguna College of Art Design.

JSFL is probably the most exciting new feature in Flash MX 2004, and it's certainly the feature we were both most excited about when we got our hands on the new version. See, there are all these things we do every day in Flash that take up loads of time—repetitive, boring grunt work, but they're such weird little things that Macromedia could never add them as features to Flash itself. So instead they added an extensibility layer and gave us the ability to develop the tools we need.

In this project, we tackle one small area of JSFL—the ability to create text effects—but what's important is the technique behind it. It's one of those "get your feet wet" projects that serves as a springboard for, well, whatever features you would like to see in Flash.

Which leads us to the absolute coolest thing about JSFL—Macromedia has done a genius thing by giving us the power to influence the Flash feature set. Flash creators have to be some of the most creative, dedicated, innovative, and hard-working individuals we've ever met, and their talents have already transformed the Web. It's going to be a cool and crazy ride seeing how you guys can apply that same vigor to extending the tool we use day in and day out.

It Works Like This

You can create text effects by using a language that is new to Flash MX 2004: JSFL, or Flash JavaScript. However, text effects are only one small part of Flash JavaScript. In addition to creating animated effects, you can use JSFL to automate repetitive actions (see the two accompanying JSFL commands on the *Flash MX 2004 Magic CD*) and even create new drawing tools that show up in the Toolbox. Here are the basic steps of the project:

1   Create a GUI for your text effect to allow users of your JSFL commands to modify the animation.

2   Create the initial code and save your original text by creating a copy of it on a new, locked guide layer with its visibility set to zero.

3   Break your text field into individual letters and convert them to symbols so that each of them can be animated.

4   Add the symbols to the Library, and then modify the letters based on properties set by the GUI.

5   Create the tweens and stagger the layers to create the effect of each letter animating one after the other.

6   Clean up the leftovers from the animation process, remove the effect, and finish the Timeline creation.

Flash JavaScript gives you the power to automate repetitive actions.

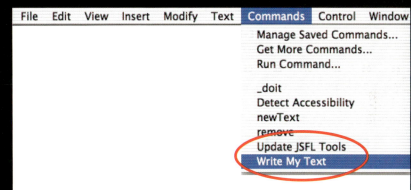

You'll learn the process to reduce the time it takes to build Flash projects.

Note: JSFL is a very dense language and we are by no means going to even scratch the surface of the language. If you like what you read here and want to learn more about JSFL, Macromedia has recently added the supporting documentation as a PDF to their website `http://download.macromedia.com/pub/documentation/en/flash/mx2004/jsapi.zip`.

Preparing to Work

To prepare for this project, you will need to do the following:

1   Copy the **Projects/11** folder to your hard drive.

2   Locate the files **Write My Text.jsfl** and **Update JSFL Tools.jsfl**.

    Write My Text.jsfl is a simple command that will create a text field on the Stage with <u>This is My Text Effect</u> typed into it. While developing the Timeline effect, you'll want to start with a fresh text field quite often. By using this command, you won't need to continually type the same text string repeatedly.

    Update JSFL Tools.jsfl tells Flash to update any of the commands or effects that are located in the **commands** or **effects** folders. Without this command, you would have to restart Flash every time you updated your Timeline effect.

3   Copy **Write My Text.jsfl** and **Update JSFL Tools.jsfl** to the Commands folder of Flash on your hard drive:

    Macintosh users—Go to User > Library > Application Support > Macromedia > Flash 2004 > en > Configuration > Commands.

    Windows users—Go to C: > Documents and Settings > user name > Local Settings > Application Data > Macromedia > Flash MX 2004 > en > Configuration > Commands.

    To use either of these commands, click on the Commands menu, where they will show up as Write My Text and Update JSFL, respectively.

4   Open your favorite text editor. All JSFL documents are text documents that are saved with a .jsfl extension.

Creating a GUI for Your Effect with XML

All JSFL effects must have a corresponding XML file that defines the behaviors of the effect. The XML file tells Flash the name of the effect; whether it belongs to a group; the legal objects for the effect to be applied to; and what, if any, user-definable parameters are used (as shown in the following figure). Without this file, your effect will not show up in the Timeline Effects menu!

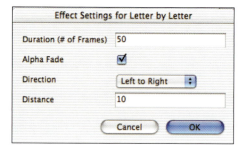

1   Create a new document in your favorite text editor.

2   Enter the Group Name that this effect is associated with.

Listing 11.1

```
<group name="">
```

All Timeline Effects XML documents must start with the group name node. You don't have to define this node; in fact, you can leave it blank (which is how most Timeline Effects XML documents are created). That is what you're going to do with this effect.

Note: If you assign a group name, this effect will show up as a hierarchical menu in the Timeline Effect menu. If no group name is selected, the effect shows up on the main menu.

3 Enter the name of the effect (directly underneath the group name node) as Letter by Letter. The name you enter here shows up in the Timeline Effects menu.

Listing 11.2

```
<effect name="Letter by Letter" />
```

4 Enter the location of the JSFL source file: letterXletter.jfsl.

Listing 11.3

```
<source file="letterXletter.jsfl" />
```

5 Enter the Allowable Object Types by setting the allow types node to text.

Listing 11.4

```
<allow types = "text" />
```

6 Enter the list of properties directly after the allow types node.

Listing 11.5

```
<properties>
 <property name="Duration (# of Frames)"
 ➥variable="duration" min="10" defaultValue="50"
 ➥type="Number" />
 <property name="Alpha Fade" variable="fade"
 ➥defaultValue="True" type="Boolean" />
 <property name="Direction" variable="direction" list="Left
 ➥to Right, Right to Left" defaultValue="0" type="Strings"
 ➥/>
 <property name="Distance" variable="distance"
 ➥defaultValue="10" type="Number" />
</properties>
```

7 Close the XML nodes by creating a closing tag (</group>) for the group name node on the last line of your XML document.

8 Save this XML file as letterXletter.xml:

Macintosh users—Go to User > Library > Application Support > Macromedia > Flash 2004 > en > Configuration > Effects.

Windows users—Go to C: > Documents and Settings > user name > Local Settings > Application Data > Macromedia > Flash MX 2004 > en > Configuration > Effects.

Creating the Initial Code to Start the Effect

With the GUI set and the user-defined parameters created, it's time to start the JSFL file. When you're starting the code for the effect, you should write several lines of code before the actual effect code. Some of this code is used for easier debugging, and some is used to reduce the amount of typing you will need to do.

1 Create a new text document and save it in the Effects folder as letterXletter.jsfl.

CAUTION

There are two folders called Effects that are created when you install Flash MX 2004. The first is located in the same folder that Flash is located in, under First Run. *Do not* put the files you create with this project in that Effects folder. Instead, locate the Effects folder where you saved the XML file from the previous section and save your JSFL file there. If you save in the wrong folder, your effect will not show up or update in the Flash IDE until the next time you start Flash.

2   Add the `executeEffect()` function.

Listing 11.6

```
function executeEffect()
{

}
```

3   Add <u>fl.enableImmediateUpdates();</u> as the first line of `executeEffect();`.

Listing 11.7

```
fl.enableImmediateUpdates();
```

Tip: JavaScript Flash can get pretty cumbersome in its syntax when you're trying to access objects and methods. To help alleviate extra typing and reduce the possibility of a spelling error slipping through, it's a good idea to create shorter, easier-to-remember references to the long JavaScript Flash names.

4   Create a reference to the effect being applied. Remember to keep it inside the curly braces for the function.

Listing 11.8

```
var myEffect = fl.activeEffect;
```

This creates a new variable called `myEffect,` which holds a reference to the current effect.

Note: One of the unfortunate and frustrating features of JSFL is its limited development environment. It's nearly impossible to do proper debugging. Basically, if something is wrong with your script, it just stops working. It won't tell you where or why; you just have to guess. You can sometimes tell where it's broken based on where the effect stops. Your best bet is to add several **trace** statements to help navigate your way through code. Trace statements in JSFL work just like they do in ActionScript; they just need prefacing with `fl`.

5   Create a reference to the current Flash Document Object Model (DOM).

Listing 11.9

```
var myDoc = fl.getDocumentDOM();
```

This reference makes it easier throughout the code to refer to the JavaScript DOM. You could get away with not writing this line and replacing every instance of `myDoc` with `fl.getDocumentDOM();`.

6   Prepare the main Timeline for your new effect by adding this code.

Listing 11.10

```
myDoc.getTimeline().insertFrames(myEffect.duration-1,
➥false);
```

With this effect, you are going to be creating an animation that exists over a set number of frames. Before (or after) applying the animation to the text, add the same number of frames to the main Timeline so that the Timeline has enough frames to accommodate the new effect. The `duration` variable created in the XML document determines the number of frames.

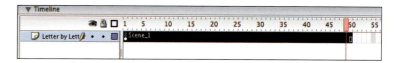

7   Save your work. Your code is now set up, and you're ready to start applying the effect to the text.

CAUTION

Unlike ActionScript 1.0, JSFL is a case-sensitive language, which means that the variable `myVar` is different than `MyVar` or `MYVAR`. Make sure that you take extra care when typing in the code contained in this chapter. If you get to the end of any step and your code isn't working the way it should, check for capitalization errors.

Saving the Original Text in an Editable Format

It's always a good idea to save an unedited version of whatever you are applying an effect to. There is no simple "remove effect" function with JSFL. This is especially true of text-based effects because text is one of the most constantly changing aspects of any Flash project.

The easiest way to save an original version of the text, should you choose to remove the effect, is to create a copy of the text on a new guide layer that is locked and has its visibility set to zero. Placing a copy of the text on a guide layer ensures that it is not exported when publishing the movie, so it doesn't add to the published movie's file size. Keeping that layer locked and invisible keeps it from getting in the way or from being removed accidentally.

1   Still inside the curly braces for the function, add the following code to open the text in Edit mode.

Listing 11.11

```
myDoc.enterEditMode("inPlace");
```

2   Add this code to select everything on the symbol's Timeline and copy it to the Clipboard.

Listing 11.12

```
myDoc.selectAll();
myDoc.clipCopy();
```

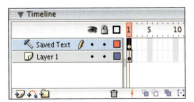

3   With everything selected, execute a `clipCopy();` function, which copies the selected object(s) to Flash's Clipboard, just as if you had pressed Ctrl+C/Cmd+C.

Listing 11.13

```
myDoc.getTimeline().addNewLayer("Saved Text", "guide",
➥true);
myDoc.getTimeline().setSelectedLayers(0);
myDoc.clipPaste(true);
```

This code adds a new layer to the Timeline and pastes the contents of the Clipboard to this new layer.

To add a new layer, use the `addNewLayer("Saved Text", "guide", true);` function. Note that the function has three arguments. The first argument is the name of the layer. The second argument is the type of layer. As mentioned earlier, this layer should be a guide layer. The third argument is a Boolean; therefore, `true` places the new layer above the currently selected layer, and `false` places the new layer below it.

To select the new layer, use the `setSelectedLayer();` function, which accepts a single argument of which layer you want to select. As with most things Flash, the first element is usually indicated by the number 0. The layer you just created was created above the current layer; therefore, it's the first layer, so it's 0.

Finally, paste the contents of the Clipboard onto this new layer with the `clipPaste();` function. `clipPaste();` also accepts just one argument—a Boolean—which determines whether the paste process should be a "paste in place" (`true`) or just a regular paste (`false`).

4   Lock the new layer and set its visibility to `false`.

Listing 11.14

```
myDoc.getTimeline().setLayerProperty("locked", true);
myDoc.getTimeline().setLayerProperty("visible", false);
```

5   At this point, save your work. If you have been working in an external text editor and don't have Flash open at this point, go ahead and open it now, then select the Update JSFL Tools from the commands menu, and then the Write My Text command. Finally, apply the effect to some text via the contextual menu or the Insert > Timeline Effect menu.

If everything is working properly, you should see your text effect opened in Edit mode, with two layers. One is a guide layer called Saved Text, and the other layer is simply called Layer 1. The Saved Text layer should be locked.

Breaking the Text Field into Individual Characters

The next step in the process is to make what is one big text field into individual characters so that they can be animated one by one.

1   Back in the JSFL file, add this code.

Listing 11.15

```
myDoc.getTimeline().setSelectedLayers(1);
```

This code selects the correct layer—which, in this case, is the layer called Layer 1—by using the `setSelectedLayers(1);` function again, this time passing the number 1 as its argument.

2   Select the correct frames on the correct layer.

Listing 11.16

```
myDoc.getTimeline().setSelectedFrames(0,0,true);
```

In this case, it's pretty easy because the Timeline has only a single frame currently. To select frames, use `setSelectedFrames(0,0,true);` the first two arguments refer to the first frame number in the selection, and the second two arguments refer to the last frame in the selection.

Note: Macromedia defines the second argument of `setSelectedFrames()` as selecting the frame "up to but not including the designated frame." What that means is if you were to select Frames 1–10, you would use the arguments 0 (the first frame in the frames array) and 11 (which would be frame 10).

3   Select the objects on the selected frames by adding this code.

Listing 11.17

```
myDoc.selectAll();
```

Because the guide layer is locked and there are no other objects on the Stage yet, it's easy to use the `selectAll();` function again to select the text.

4   Make each letter its own object and place each of those objects on its own layer.

Listing 11.18

```
myDoc.breakApart();
myDoc.distributeToLayers();
```

This sounds like it could be difficult but, in fact, it is really easy to do, requiring just two commands: `breakApart();`, which breaks a text field into individual letters, and `distributeToLayers();`, which takes all selected objects on the Stage and puts each of them in its own layer. You get some really nice built-in benefits with these two features that make development smoother. The first benefit is that `breakApart();`

automatically leaves each "broken apart" object selected, playing right into `distributeToLayers()`. The second benefit is that `distributeToLayers()` automatically names the newly created layers, either with the symbol name of the object or, in the case of text, the value of the text.

5 Delete the extra layer with the `deleteLayer(1);` function.

Listing 11.19

```
myDoc.getTimeline().deleteLayer(1);
```

In addition to the built-in freebies you get with `distributeToLayers()`, you get one often-undesirable side effect. All of the objects that you distributed previously were on a layer called Layer 1. That layer still exists, but it doesn't have content on it; therefore, you must delete that layer for the rest of the effect to work properly. There's no real way to know which layer number this empty layer is. You could write more code to determine which layer it is, but in this case, it's much easier to run the code and just look at the position of Layer 1.

6 Deselect the objects on the Stage.

Listing 11.20

```
myDoc.selectNone();
```

Make sure you deselect the objects at the end of most steps. If you don't, it's easy to forget that you have things selected and start applying actions inadvertently.

7 Save and test your movie. Follow the same steps you have been for saving and testing.

At this stage, your effect should end with your text symbol open in Edit mode, each letter having its own layer and the guide layer with the original text still on it.

Converting Each Letter to a Symbol

In this section, you will loop through all the letters on the Stage and convert each of them to a new symbol.

1 Create two new variables to keep track of the current layer's object and the current elements.

Listing 11.21

```
var curLayers = myDoc.getTimeline().layers;
var curElements = new Array();
```

The variable `curLayers` is a reference to the document layers, which means it contains such information as length, or how many layers are in the current Timeline. The other variable, `curElements`, is a new `Array` object that you'll use later to hold a reference to all the current elements on a given layer.

2   Loop through each layer of the Timeline.

Listing 11.22

```
for (var i=1; i < curLayers.length; i++) {
}
```

Using the `curLayers.length` property, you can create a `for-in` loop to loop through each layer on the Timeline. Usually you start with 0 as the first element to loop through. In this case, though, layer 0 is the layer with the saved original text on it. You don't want to change that, so the loop should start with 1. After you have written this code, all remaining steps in this section will occur between the `for` loop's curly braces {}.

3   Set the first element of `curElements` to the first object of the selected layer.

Listing 11.23

```
curElements[0] = curLayers[i].frames[0].elements[0];
```

Up until now, you have been explicitly selecting frames, layers, and objects one command at a time. For selecting the objects in this step, you're going to combine those three steps into one. Don't forget that this step should appear between the {} of the `for-in` loop.

Note: Basically, an *element* refers to anything on the Stage. For instance, if you have a one-layer, one-frame movie, you can still have multiple "elements" on that one frame. You could have several buttons, some text, a background image, and a bitmap. Each of those things would be considered an element.

---

4   Set the currently selected item to `curElements`.

Listing 11.24

```
myDoc.selection = curElements;
```

Use the `selection` property to set the current selection of Flash equal to the element in `curElements`.

5   Create a name for the symbol.

Listing 11.25

```
var symbolName = myEffect.effectName + "_" + i;
```

If you don't create a name for the symbol, you might encounter Library conflicts. The simplest option is for each letter to have a symbol name that has the same name as the effect with an incremental number to avoid conflict. Do this by accessing the effect's name `myEffect.effectName` and then appending the variable `i`. That variable, of course, represents a number.

6   Convert the current selection to a symbol.

Listing 11.26

```
myDoc.convertToSymbol("graphic", symbolName, "center");
```

convertToSymbol() accepts three arguments. The first argument determines the type of symbol, graphic, button, or movie clip. The second argument is the name of the symbol. Finally, the third argument is the registration point—in this case, center.

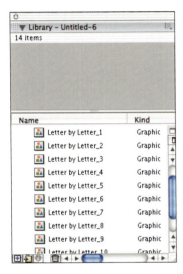

7   Deselect the current object.

Listing 11.27

```
myDoc.selectNone();
```

CAUTION

Make sure you deselect the current object; otherwise, each subsequent symbol will contain the previous one. For example, if you were applying this effect to the word *THE*, your first symbol would be *T*, the second would be *TH*, and the third would be *THE*.

8   Save your work.

Adding the Symbols to the Library

This section is a bit confusing because you're going to modify existing code, inserting lines between lines that are already created. Basically, you want to create a library folder to hold all your letter symbols. Truth be told, you don't *need* to, but the Library can get messy pretty quickly when you're using Timeline effects.

1   The first thing you want to do is create a name for your new library item. You can do this by adding the following line of code before the for-in loop you created in the previous section.

Listing 11.28

```
var effectLibrary = myEffect.effectName + "_assets";
```

The name of the library folder should be related to the name of the effect—in this case, Letter by Letter_assets. This doesn't create the folder yet; it just creates a name that will be used to create the folder.

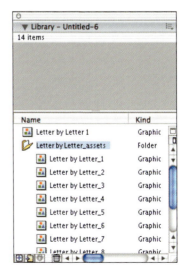

2   Create the new Library folder.

Listing 11.29

```
myDoc.library.addNewItem("folder", effectLibrary);
```

The addNewItem() function accepts two arguments. The first argument is the type of Library element; here it's a folder. The second is the name of that Library item.

Note: Until now, most of the code has dealt with myDoc.getTimeline(), but now that you're dealing with the Library, getTimeline() is replaced with library. This just indicates to Flash that you want to deal with the Library to execute the effect, not the Timeline.

3   You want to be able to move the symbols created in the for-in loop in to the folder that was just created in the library. To do this add the next line of code to the for-in loop before the myDoc.selectNone(); line.

Listing 11.30

```
var curLayers = myDoc.getTimeline().layers;
var curElements = new Array();

var effectLibrary = myEffect.effectName + "_assets";
myDoc.library.addNewItem("folder", effectLibrary);

for(var i=1; i<curLayers.length; i++) {
   curElements[0] = curLayers[1].frames[0].elements[0];
   myDoc.selection = curElements;

   var symbolName = myEffect.effectName + "_" + i;
   myDoc.convertToSymbol("graphic", symbolName, "center");
   myDoc.library.moveToFolder
   ➥(effectLibrary, myEffect.effectName + "_" + i);
   myDoc.selectNone();
}
```

4   Save and test your work. When testing your effect this time, you should see a new folder in the Library called "Letter by Letter_assets."

Handling the Direction Option

Now that you have symbols for each letter set up, and each symbol is on its own layer, it's time to deal with the animation. The first step is to determine what direction the animation should move in. The user gets to set this as an option, either left to right or right to left. This is one of the options set up in the XML GUI created earlier in this project.

1   To set the animation direction add this if statement to the JSFL file immediately after the for-in loop you used to create the letter symbols.

Listing 11.31

```
if(myEffect.direction == "Left to Right") {
  myEffect.distance *= -1;
}
```

Check the direction variable that is set via the XML GUI. To access the XML set variables, use myEffect.*variableName*—in this case, myEffect.direction. The code will check to see if Left to Right is true. If so, it changes another XML variable, distance, to whatever its original value was times –1.

2   Save your work.

Applying the Parameters to Each Letter

The next step is by far the most complex in this project. There's a lot of code to go through. Now it's time to loop through each letter and apply the options to it. The options in this effect are the distance the letter needs to travel and whether it should fade in.

The tricky part comes in dealing with the fact that this is animation. If you apply the alpha and distance parameters to the objects now and then create new keyframes and animate, you must select the new keyframe and remove the changes initially made. Because of this, before you apply the parameters to the letter symbols, you're going to create the keyframes.

1 Determine the length of each tween. To do this, insert this code before the if statement you just created.

Listing 11.32

```
var tweenLength = Math.floor((myEffect.duration-1)/
➡curLayers.length);
```

Although you won't be applying the tween to the Timeline just yet, it's important to know how long the tween should be. You determine the length of the tween by taking the overall length of the animation (myEffect.duration) divided by the total number of letters to animate (curLayers.length).

2 Create the for loop. This loop should be placed after the if statement you created. The remainder of the code in this section will be enclosed in this for loop, which loops through all the layers to select the objects on each layer.

Listing 11.33

```
for(var i=1; i<curLayers.length; i++) {
}
```

3 Select the current layer. To select the current layer, use setSelectedLayers(), passing i as the argument.

Listing 11.34

```
myDoc.getTimeline().setSelectedLayers(i);
```

4 Insert frames into the effect.

Listing 11.35

```
myDoc.getTimeline().insertFrames(myEffect.duration-1,
➡false, 0);
```

When you insert the frames, every layer must extend to the end of the effect; otherwise, letters will disappear as the animation plays. The total length of the effect is held in the XML variable myEffect.duration. Because the myEffect.duration is human readable, you must subtract the total amount by 1.

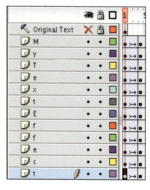

5 Insert a keyframe by converting the last frame of the animation to a key frame with the convertToKeyframes() function, passing it the tweenLength parameter.

Listing 11.36

```
myDoc.getTimeline().convertToKeyframes(tweenLength);
```

6   Select the first frame of the current layer.

Listing 11.37

```
myDoc.getTimeline().currentFrame = 0;
```

7   Select the objects on the first frame of the current layer.

Listing 11.38

```
curElements[0] = curLayers[i].frames[0].elements[0];
myDoc.selection = curElements;
```

This should look familiar because in the previous `for-in` loop, you used the `curElements` variable to keep track of the objects on the Stage, in the selected frame of the selected layer.

8   Move the currently selected letter symbol.

Listing 11.39

```
myDoc.moveSelectionBy({x:myEffect.distance, y:0});
```

Now is the time you're actually going to move the selected object on the Stage using the `moveSelectionBy()` function. To use this function, you pass along a special argument contained within a pair of braces {}. The arguments to pass are X and Y values in this format: `{x:myEffect.distance, y:0}`. Specifically in this example, `myEffect.distance` is the number of pixels that the letter should move as determined by the user in the XML GUI. Y is unused in this project.

9   Apply the alpha fade to the currently selected symbol.

Listing 11.40

```
if(myEffect.fade == true) {
 myDoc.setInstanceAlpha(0);
}
```

You start by checking the value of `myEffect.fade`. If that value is `true`, then the currently selected item has its alpha set to 0 by using `setInstanceAlpha(0)`.

10   Save and test.

Creating the Animation of Each Letter

The keyframes are set, the instance properties are set, and it's time to make things move. Creating the tween isn't all that difficult; the hard part comes from creating the staggered effect so that each layer animates one after another, instead of all at once.

1   Create the motion tween for each layer by changing the property of the selected frame via `setFrameProperty()` and passing it three arguments.

Listing 11.41

```
myDoc.getTimeline().setFrameProperty("tweenType", "motion",
➡0);
```

`tweenType` indicates that the property of the frame to change is its tween type. Use `motion` to set the type of tween. This code goes after the `if` statement you just created, but still within the `for` loop.

2   Stagger the layer animation by first cutting the frames of the selected layer using the `cutFrames()` function, passing two arguments.

Listing 11.42

```
myDoc.getTimeline().cutFrames(0,tweenLength);
myDoc.getTimeline().pasteFrames( ((i-1)*tweenLength), (((i-
➡1)*tweenLength) + tweenLength));
```

The first argument is the start frame, or 0, and the second argument is the end frame, or the total length of the animation as it currently is.

After you've cut the tween, paste it using the `pasteFrames()` function. Like `cutFrames()`, `pasteFrames()` accepts two arguments: the start frame to paste into and the end frame to paste into. To create the stagger effect, ensure that each subsequent layer's first frame matches the previous layer's last frame. To determine exactly what those frame numbers are, multiply the `tweenLength` by the current layer (subtract 1), as determined by the loop. That gives you the start frame. The end frame is determined through the same formula, but adding the `tweenLength` amount to it.

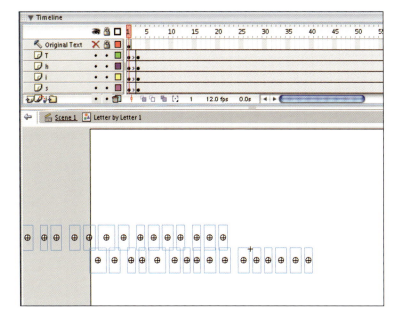

3   Delete stray frames by using `clearKeyFrames(tweenLength);` for any layer greater than Layer 2.

Listing 11.43

```
if(i>2) {
myDoc.getTimeline().clearKeyframes(tweenLength);
}
```

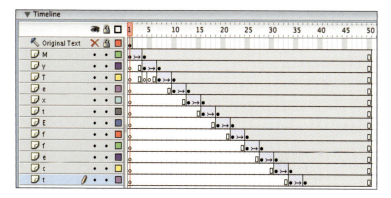

4   Lock the currently selected layer. This step isn't wholly necessary, but locking the layer via the `setLayerProperty()` function helps prevent the animation from being altered accidentally.

Listing 11.44

```
myDoc.getTimeline().setLayerProperty("locked", true);
```

5   Save your work.

Cleaning Up the Effect's Timeline and Returning the User to the Main Timeline

This is the last step for creating the effect. Most users won't want to see the guts of the effect, so you'll want to exit Edit mode. Also, depending on the effect, you might want to alter the effect to play only once (the default is to loop). The code here goes after the `for-in` loop.

1   Deselect the objects on the Timeline using `selectNone()` and changing the current frame of the Timeline effect to the first frame with `currentFrame = 0;`. You're done with the `for` loop now; this code goes right after it.

Listing 11.45

```
myDoc.selectNone();
myDoc.getTimeline().currentFrame = 0;
```

2   Exit Edit mode and return to the main Timeline.

Listing 11.46

```
myDoc.exitEditMode();
```

3   Set the play type of the effect. For the most part, you won't need to, but for this effect, you only want the text to animate once. Use the `setElementProperty()` function to change the `loop` behavior to `play once`.

Listing 11.47

```
myDoc.setElementProperty("loop", "play once");
```

4   Save and test. You should have a fully functional effect, at least in terms of applying the effect.

Removing the Effect

There's one last step to completing a Timeline effect, and that's giving the user the option to remove it. Fortunately, removing the effect is much easier than creating it. The task consists mostly of deleting layers and changing the Saved Text layer back to a visible, unlocked, and normal layer.

1   Create the `removeEffect()` function.

Listing 11.48

```
function removeEffect()
{
}
```

The code in the following steps will go inside this function.

2   Create a reference to the Flash DOM.

Listing 11.49

```
var myDoc = fl.getDocumentDOM();
```

3   Open the Timeline effect symbol in Edit mode.

Listing 11.50

```
myDoc.enterEditMode("inPlace");
```

4   Determine the total number of layers in the effect.

Listing 11.51

```
var totalLayers = myDoc.getTimeline().layers.length;
➥(myDoc.getTimeline().layers[1].frames.length) - 1;
```

5   Delete all animated layers using another `for-in` loop.

Listing 11.52

```
for(var i=1; i<totalLayers; i++) {
  myDoc.getTimeline().deleteLayer(i);
}
```

The only layer without animation will be the guide layer that you created to save an unedited version of the text.

6   Return the Saved Text layer to its original state.

Listing 11.53

```
myDoc.getTimeline().setSelectedLayers(0);
myDoc.getTimeline().setLayerProperty("locked", false);
myDoc.getTimeline().setLayerProperty("visible", true);
myDoc.getTimeline().setLayerProperty("layerType",
➡"normal");
```

First, select layer 1 with the `setSelectedLayers()` function. Then change the `locked`, `visible` and `layerType` properties of the layer with `setLayerProperty()`. This code follows the `for` statement from the previous step.

7   Exit Edit mode.

Listing 11.54

```
myDoc.selectNone();
myDoc.exitEditMode();
```

8   Finally remove the folder containing the letter symbol assets that was created earlier.

Listing 11. 55

```
myDoc.library.deleteItem(fl.activeEffect.effectName +
➡"_assets");
```

9   Save your work.

Now Try This

By now you've learned how to create a simple text effect using the new JSFL scripting language. The GUI you created for your text effect allows users of your JSFL commands to modify certain aspects of the animation. Once the initial code was created, you broke the text field into individual letters so that each of them could be converted to symbols and modified for easy animation.

Here are some ideas on how to apply the skills you've learned or use the project you've completed in other ways:

- Add a control to change the easing of the animation.

- Have the letters start from a different horizontal position as well as vertical.

- Add an additional level of complexity to the `removeEffect()` function and have it also delete the Library items created with the `executeEffect()` function.

- Create a full Flash-based GUI so as to give the end user the ability to preview the effect before applying it.

- Add the ability to change the color of the text.

PROJECT 12

Developing Interfaces for
for Pocket PCs

Bill Spencer

Bill Spencer is the
Founder and CEO of
TheUnityProject.com, as
well as the Founder of
Popedeflash.com, the first
Flash community dedicat-
ed to 3D.

I have been longtime friends with the guys at relevare.com and loved the interface they came
up with as a simple yet elegant solution for device interfaces. During the last few years I have
seen a ton of products come out for devices but nothing as elegant or as ingenious as the relevare interfaces. That got me thinking: "What could I do to spur people on to create new and
unusual interfaces that are lightweight and functional?"

I love the use of color and believe that people should be able to navigate within a few easy
click or taps of where or what they want. The nested approach of a navigation makes it simple
for the first-time visitor to see everything available at a glance, and the return visitor can go
back to a nested area quickly. It's my passion to make functional interfaces that are artistic in
nature. I hope this project will inspire those who work with interfaces something new to try.

It Works Like This

Have you ever wanted to develop interfaces for devices but just didn't know where to start with such a small space? In this project you come face-to-face with the little giant of device interface design and create a user-friendly UI in no time flat. Here are the basic steps for this project:

1 Use Macromedia's template for the iPAQ 5440 Pocket PC to develop a standalone player delivery product.

2 Animate the entire screen, which makes the interface fun and whimsical, by using an array in ActionScript.

3 Make the interface intuitive by employing a set of nested buttons by which to navigate.

The iPAQ's small stage makes design a challenge.

But with some ingenuity, the resulting interface is small,

Preparing to Work

To prepare for this project, you will need to do the following:

1 Copy the **Projects/12** folder from the CD to your hard drive.

2 Open **Device interface.fla** and take a look what you'll be building. Close it when you're finished.

> **Note:** If you need to dive deeper into device development, check out Macromedia's website at http://www.macromedia.com/devnet/ devices/. Also, be sure to check out *Flash Enabled: Flash Design and Development for Devices* (New Riders Publishing, 2002), which is a great resource on the subject.

Setting Up the Stage

Before you start creating the interface, you need to understand the spaces you're dealing with. Because the Flash Player for the Pocket PC is the most common interface on the market today, it is the focus in this project.

1 Choose New > Templates > Mobile Devices > iPAQ 5440. You should now be looking at a Stage with dimensions set to 240×268.

> **Note:** Device interfaces are small cramped spaces and there is no standard screen size; stage areas range from 229×175 up to 240×320 on the Pocket PC alone. Macromedia recommends that you develop to a 230×250 pixel size for delivery to Internet Explorer for Pocket PC.

2 Hide the top guide layer, named Device, which contains the template image of the device you are working on.

3 Insert a new folder on the timeline. To do this, right-click or Ctrl+click and select insert folder from the menu. Name the new folder <u>interface</u>. Create a new layer and name it <u>panel</u>, and rename the layer content to be <u>sliding interface</u>. Move them both into the interface folder with the Panel layer above the Sliding Interface layer.

4 Save your work.

Creating the Background Assets

Now that you've laid the groundwork, you are going to create the base element of the project. You will be using the available tools in Flash to create everything. So with that, let's get started.

1 Select the first frame in the Sliding Interface layer. Choose the Rectangle tool and draw a square on the Stage. Set the stroke to None and the fill to R204, G82, B0.

2 Resize the square on the Stage to match that of the movie: 240×268 pixels. Set the X and Y values of the rectangle to 0 by using the Properties inspector.

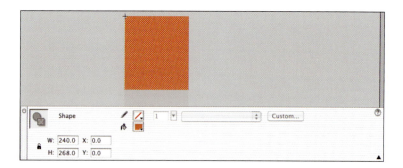

3 Select the rectangle, and press the F8 key or select Modify > Convert to Symbol. Give the new movie clip a name of <u>background</u>.

4 Copy the new movie clip to the Clipboard.

5 Select the first frame of the Panel layer. Paste the movie clip in place using the Paste in Place command.

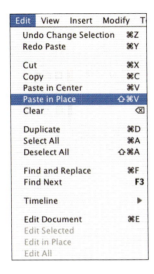

6 Select the movie clip you just pasted into the Panel layer, Ctrl-click/right-click on it and select Duplicate Symbol. In the dialog box, name the duplicate movie slide. With the movie clip slide still selected, give it an instance name of slide using the Properties inspector.

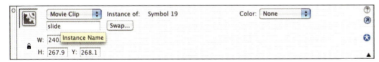

7 Save your work.

Designing the Sliding Background

You are now going to create the sliding Stage background. To do this you need to do a little math first. You know that the current Stage assets are 240×268, but let's say that you have four different areas that you want to navigate to and that each of those areas have four areas to navigate to as well. Your background will need to be 4×240 (960 pixels wide) and 4×268 (1072 pixels high).

1 Select the Stage and set the movie to be 960 pixels wide and 1072 pixels high. This will make creating the interface much easier because you will be able to see all of the working area.

2 Hide and lock the Panel layer in the Timeline. Select the movie clip on the Sliding Interface layer and double-click on the movie clip so you can edit the fill.

3 Select the fill, and copy and paste it to the Stage by using Ctrl+D/Opt+D. Select a new color of your choice for the new fill on the Stage. I used a nice shade of Burgundy R94, G31, B28.

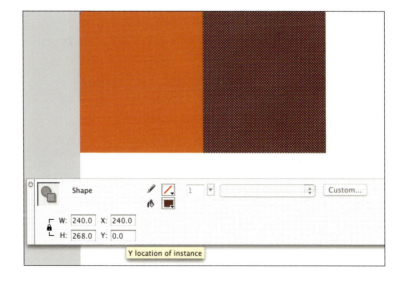

4   In the Properties inspector, set the registration point of the new fill to X: 240 and Y: 0. The registration point is located at the upper-left corner of the fill. This will be important later on.

Notice that Flash sets the default registration point of symbols to the upper-left corner unless specified by the user. This is a good thing to know when you need to start lining things up.

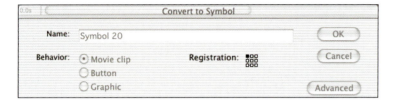

5   Now repeat the process of duplicating the shape to the Stage, changing its color, and lining up the shapes side by side. You will need to do this a total of 14 more times.

The RGB values for all 16 blocks are as follows (left to right and top to bottom):

First Row: (204, 182, 0), (94, 31, 28), (0, 95, 140), (0, 102, 0)

Second Row: (255, 102, 0), (123, 40, 36), (0, 112, 166), (0, 151, 0)

Third Row: (255, 152, 83), (151, 50, 45), (0, 124, 185), (0, 179,0)

Fourth Row: (255, 166, 106), (197, 66, 58), (0, 136, 202), (0, 202, 0)

The idea is to fill the Stage area. Be sure that the blocks do not overlap one another but rest side by side. This means that once you have created the block and changed its color, you will need to use the Properties inspector to set the placement of the block.

To do this, you need to do some more math. You know the stage is 240×268 and you know that the first block's X and Y registration is set to 0,0. Make sure you set each of the blocks to the correct X and Y positions (refer to the values below):

First Row: (0, 0), (240, 0), (480, 0), (720, 0)

Second Row: (0, 268), (240, 268), (480, 268), (720, 268)

Third Row: (0, 536), (240, 536), (480, 536), (720, 536)

Fourth Row: (0, 804), (240, 804), (480, 804), (720, 804)

6   Save your work.

Creating the Navigation

The navigation consists mostly of buttons that are created by copying the squares that make up the background you created in the preceding section. Buttons are special for the Pocket PC because they are activated by either the user's finger or stylus on the touch-based screen (you do not have a cursor that you can use or rollover state's, like with a mouse). Therefore, it is important to make the button-hit area large enough for the user to be able to select it using a stylus. A down state in the button is a usable asset, but you will not be utilizing this feature because the interface will be scrolling as soon as the button is selected. Another method of navigation you can use for development is the d-pad (digital pad—a 5-way cursor navigation located at the bottom center of the Pocket PC). This responds to the left, right, up, and down arrow keys as well as pressing in equals enter.

Tip: You can create a single "invisible button" (a button with only the hit area) and re-use it on the Stage. This is a good practice because, in most cases, it will help keep file size down.

---

1   Select all the blocks you created in the preceding section and copy them to the Clipboard.

2. Create two new layers; name the top layer <u>actions</u>, the second layer <u>buttons</u>, and rename the layer at the bottom with the background squares <u>squares</u>. Paste the blocks you just copied to the clip board into the layer <u>buttons</u>. Do this by placing your cursor in the first keyframe of the layer buttons and then using the right-click (PC), Ctrl+click (Mac) method paste the blocks into the layer. Lock the layer squares so we will not modify them in a later step.

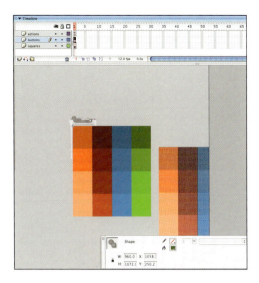

3   With all the blocks still selected, change the object size to 240×268 in the Properties inspector.

4   Select the very first block in the group of objects you just resized.

5   Using F8 or Modify > Create Symbol, make the block a button. Give it a name of 1. Do the same for all the other blocks, starting with the next block to the right of the block you just changed into a button. When you are finished, you should have 16 buttons in the buttons layer.

6   Save your work.

Adding the ActionScript to Make It Work

Now for the easy part—yes, that's right, the easy part. All that makes this puppy run is 18 lines of simple code on the main movie clip and one line of code on each button to call the array you will build within the 18 lines of code. The following image shows the complete code.

```
this.destX=0;
    this.destY=0;
    // create and array to hold the x positions of the 16 destination locations.
    arrXValues = new Array(0, -240, -480, -720, 0, -240, -480, -690, 0, -240, -480, -720, 0, -240, -480, -720);
    // create and array to hold the 7 positions of the 16 destination locations.
    arrYValues = new Array(0, 0, 0, 0, -268, -268, -268, -268, -536, -536, -536, -536, -804, -804, -804, -804);
    // set a variable for the percent to travel to the destination for each frame that the code executes
    percent = .10;
    // create a function to capture the button events
    function positionNav(_location) {
        // set the destination x and y based on the location number
        this.destX = arrXValues[_location-1];
        this.destY = arrYValues[_location-1];
    }

this.onEnterFrame = function() {
    // Delares the function
    if ((this._x != this.destX) || (this._y != this.destY)) {
        // enters this conditional if it has not reached the desination
        // set a variable equal to the distance needed to travel in the x direction
        var xDist = this.destX - this._x
        // set a variable equal to the distance needed to travel in the y direction
        var yDist = this.destY - this._y;
        // move a percent of the distance from the current position to the destination
        this._x += percent*xDist;
        this._y += percent*yDist;
    }
```

1   Go to the main Timeline. On the Sliding Interface layer, select the movie clip containing the sliding background. Give it the instance name menu in the Properties inspector.

2   With the movie clip you just named menu still selected, double click to show the movie clip's timeline. Place your cursor in the first keyframe of the Actions layer which should be located at the top of the timeline. With the cursor in the first keyframe, open the Actions panel.

The first 9 lines of code set the movie clip up by declaring all the variables, arrays, and functions. The second half (the remaining 9 lines of code) execute the array positions you declared in the first half of the code.

3   Start by adding the variables. In the newly created layer named actions, select the first frame, open the Actions panel, and add the following code.

Listing 12.1

```
this.destX=0;
this.destY=0;
```

This sets the initial destination X and Y to 0.

Note: If you prefer to insert the entire code at once, use the code named **complete_code.txt** from the **Projects/12/Code listings** folder you copied to your hard drive during "Preparing to Work."

4   Create an array to hold the X positions of the 16 destination locations.

Listing 12.2

```
arrXValues = new Array(0, -240, -480, -720, 0, -240,
➥-480, -720, 0, -240, -480, -720, 0, -240, -480,
➥-720);
```

The way this works is that you declare the variable name, arrXValues, and then say that the arrXValues variable equals an array of numbers, which are the 16 different X positions that can be set. These numbers can be any pixel you want on the Stage. The way you call them is simply by using the position number they are set to in the array. For instance, position 1 in this array equals 0, position 2 equals –240, and so on.

5   Create an array to hold the Y positions of the 16 destination locations.

Listing 12.3

```
arrYValues = new Array(0, 0, 0, 0, -268, -268, -268,
➥-268, -536, -536, -536, -536, -804, -804, -804,
➥-804);
```

6   Set a variable for the percent of the total distance to travel between the current location and the final destination for each frame that the code executes.

Listing 12.4

```
percent = .10;
```

This controls the speed the of the menu movie clip's movement. If you jack up the percent to .50, you would move the clip five times as fast as set at .10.

7   Now you need to create a function to capture the button events, so add this code.

Listing 12.5

```
function positionNav(_location) {
```

Notice that the selected location is passed into the function as _location.

8   Add this code.

Listing 12.6

```
        this.destX = arrXValues[_location-1];
        this.destY = arrYValues[_location-1];
    }
}
```

This sets the destination of X and Y based on the location passed into the function.

9   Add the enterFrame event.

Listing 12.7

```
this.onEnterFrame = function(){
```

This checks each frame to see if the destination X or Y positions have changed. If either has, then it calls the positionNav function that you just created.

10   Check to see whether the movie clip is currently sitting at the destination X and Y positions:

Listing 12.8

```
    if ((this._x != this.destX) || (this._y !=
➥this.destY)) {
```

This creates a variable for the distance needed to travel for the X and Y positions.

11   Set a variable equal to the distance needed to travel in the X direction. Then set another variable equal to the distance needed to travel in the Y direction.

Listing 12.9

```
        var xDist = this.destX - this._x
        var yDist = this.destY - this._y;
```

12   Set the new X and Y positions equal to the percent you set earlier by multiplying by the total distance between the current position and the destination. Then, once again, close out the conditional statement and the `enterFrame` event handler.

Listing 12.10

```
        this._x += percent*xDist;
        this._y += percent*yDist;
    }
}
```

The command on the buttons will call the function you created and will use the arrays to set the position of the movie clip.

13   Add the code to the buttons. Double-click on the Menu instance of the background movie clip and select the first button in the upper-left corner. Add this code in the Actions panel.

Listing 12.11

```
on(release) {
        positionNav(1);
    }
```

This code simply calls the array you created on the movie clip and tells it to go to Position 1, which is X = 0 and Y = 0.

14   Add the same code to each of the other buttons, but be sure to change the position number to the appropriate array position.

This is where the matrix mentioned earlier helps out. The buttons should be color coordinated, and the numbers should run left to right and from top to bottom.

15   Save your work.

Building an Easy-to-Navigate User Interface

You have all your scripts and buttons created; now you need to create and arrange the buttons in such a way that your end users are able to navigate with ease. You can create navigation hints using color and shades of the same color to denote a path of navigation, use positioning and scale of the buttons, or use the most common of all navigation paradigms: words. In this section, you'll use all three.

1   Select the first button in the upper-left corner and set it aside. Because it represents the very first, or home block, you will not need this for this step.

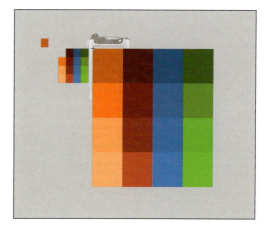

2 Double-click on the button below the button that represents the home position. Create a new layer in the button and name it <u>text</u>. In the new layer add the word <u>careers</u>. Use either a pixel font or the new alias text feature in MX 2004. The new alias text feature can produce the same effect as pixel fonts. Now repeat the process to the buttons below adding the word <u>more</u>. I chose to use standard 07_54, which is a pixel font I downloaded from `www.miniml.com`, but you can choose either option.

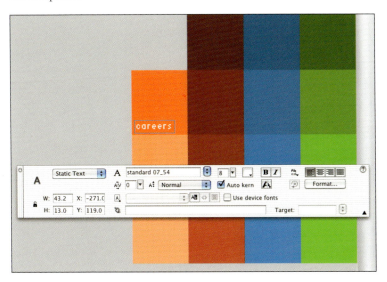

Note: The Alias Text button in the Properties inspector lets you render text so that it appears more readable at small sizes. This feature supports static, dynamic, and input text at the Flash Player 7 or higher level and only static text in the earlier versions.

Only the text selected on the stage is effected (not the entire document) when this feature is used. This means each separate area of text will need the feature applied to it to be enabled.

Basic guides include the following:

- Text below 8 points may not appear clear even with alias text selected.

- Sans serif text, such as Arial or Helvetica, appear clear at small sizes rather than serif text.

- Some type styles like italic or bold can make readability poor at small sizes.

- Text in some cases appears smaller in Flash than it does in other applications at the same point size.

Flash MX 2004 enables pixel-snapping—select View > Snapping > Snap to Pixels. For the most legible text on small screens use pixel fonts set on whole pixel registration points (for example 25.0 instead of 25.7).

I used standard 07_54, which I downloaded from `www.minimal.com`, but you can use whatever pixel font you like.

Note: Flash MX 2004 enables pixel-snapping. Simply select View > Snapping > Snap to Pixels. For the most legible text on small screens, use pixel fonts set on whole pixel registration points.

3 Add the word <u>gallery</u> to the next button at the top right. Then add the word <u>more</u> to the buttons below it.

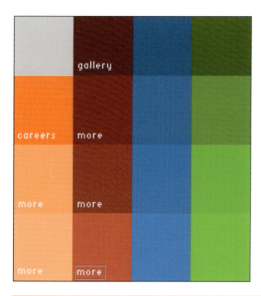

Note: Nesting the buttons not only indicates the importance of the information to the end user but it makes it much more accessible on return visits. The inspiration of combining color and scale, and nesting buttons as a navigation scheme, originated from relevare.com. The difference is that Relevare used the z-space to zoom deeper into information.

4 Add the words <u>about us</u> on the button to the right of the last series of buttons you just changed, and then add the words <u>vision</u>, <u>clients</u>, and <u>case study</u> to the buttons below about us in that order.

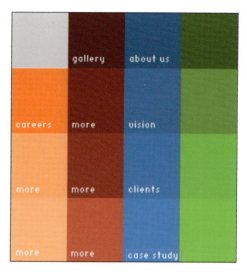

5 Add the words <u>Services</u>, <u>Marketing</u>, <u>Oversight</u>, and <u>Consulting</u> to the last row of buttons in the order given from top to bottom.

6 Select the bottom button in the second column and using the Transform tool Ctrl+T (PC) or Cmd+T (Mac), copy and apply a transformation of 35.0 percent to the button. To do this in the transform dialog select Constrain to keep the scale of the new button in proportion on both sides set the transform to 35.0 percent. Select the Copy and apply button at the bottom right closest to the center at the bottom. A new smaller copy of the button will appear.

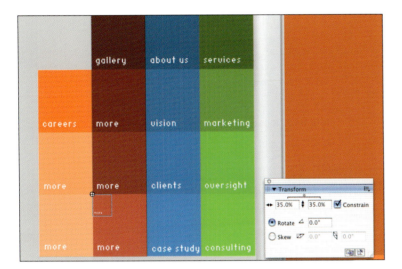

7 Take the transformed button and move it up to the left-hand corner of the third button in the second column. Selecting both the transformed button you just created and moved, as well as the button below it, use the same method as the previous step and copy and apply a transform of 35.0 percent to these buttons. Repeat this process to the top button.

8   Using the following figure as a guide, repeat step 7 to set all the but-
    tons into place. Use the first button, which represents the home area
    as your back button, to return to the main menu. You may stylize it as
    I have by editing the button into the shape of a triangle or another
    shape of your own choice. Set the color to hex #ffffff and set the alpha
    of the button to 25 percent. Now duplicate the button and place it on
    every panel as a return button as pictured.

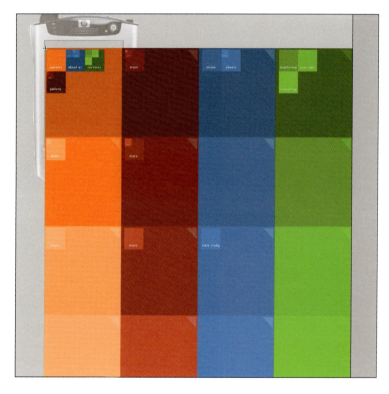

9   Save your work.

Creating the Sliding Panel

A *sliding panel* is another simple way to create space on a crowded Stage. In
it, you can store empty movie clips that various forms, graphics, and more
can be loaded into. This gives the end user the ability to keep the information handy but still be able to view the rest of the screen on command.

1   Go to the main timeline and hide and lock the Sliding Background
    layer to prevent any unnecessary modifications. Now unhide (reveal)
    the Panel layer.

2   Double-click the panel movie clip on the Stage. Select the top portion
    of the fill object with the Selection tool by dragging it across the
    screen. The area you capture needs to be 10 pixels high and 240 pixels
    wide. Make the rulers visible (if they aren't already) by choosing View
    > Rulers, and watch the vertical ruler as you drag across the screen to
    help you make your 10-pixel-high selection.

    This may take a few tries before you get it. You can see if you have the
    right size in the Properties inspector, or you can use the Info panel.

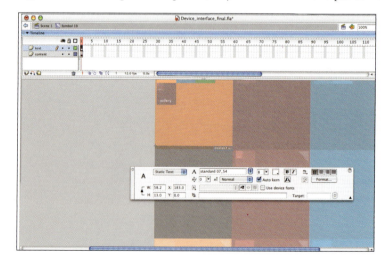

3   Once you have the area selected, create a button by pressing the F8 key and naming it <u>drag button</u>.

4   Set the color attribute in the Properties inspector to tint and select hex #999999 and a tint amount of 78 percent. Select the remaining portion of the sliding panel on the stage and set its color to hex #999999. Change the name of the layer from Layer1 to <u>content</u>.

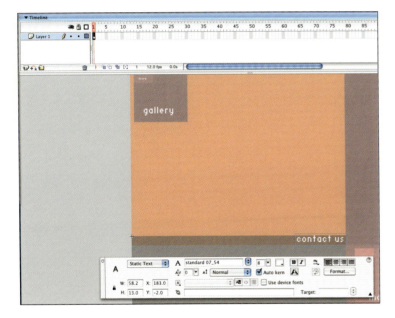

5   Add a new layer and name it <u>text</u>. Add the words <u>contact us</u> in the new layer. Make sure the new layer with the text in it sits above the layer content with the button and the background. Adding the text to the layer will indicate to the end user that there is an interface here and not just a design element. This gives you more space, with little to no footprint.

6   Add this code in the Actions panel of the button.

Listing 12.12

```
on (press) {startDrag("_root.slide",false, 0, 0, 0, 258);
}
on (release) {stopDrag();
}
```

This first action causes the sliding panel to begin dragging when the user selects the button. This action also stops the sliding panel from moving when the end user releases the button.

7   Select the slide movie clip and set its position to X: 0 and Y: 258.

8   Reset the Stage size to the original 240×268 pixel size it was in the beginning of the project.

9   Save your work and F12 to test your file. There are many nuances to delivering SWF files to devices, to get a better understanding of what they are go to http://www.macromedia.com/devnet/devices/ and download the latest development kit from Macromedia. Another great resource for developing device applications is www.pocketpcflash.net.

Now Try This

The project you just finished showed you how to develop a highly interactive but lightweight interface and output it to a small screen.

Here are some ideas on how to apply the skills you've learned or use the project you've completed in other ways:

- Create a photo gallery or a navigation bar for you website.

- Show the organizational structure of your company in an intuitive, easy-to-understand manner.

- Produce a standalone projector. In order to do that, you will need to purchase the projector license from Macromedia. You can, however, scale this file to deliver it via HTML through Internet Explorer.

INDEX

W

websites, creating in Flash, 4, 13
windowless mode, browser support, 35
Word Wrap feature, 99
wrapping text, 99

X-Y-Z

XML
    creating GUIs, 134–135
    designing container files for information
      display systems, 124–125
    loading data, 130
XML connection component, 130
XML schema, 124

www.informit.com

Voices that Matter™

VIEW CART
search ▶
▸ Registration already a member? Log in. ▸ Book Registration

web development | design | photoshop | new media | 3-D | server technologies

OUR AUTHORS

PRESS ROOM

EDUCATORS

ABOUT US

CONTACT US

You already know that New Riders brings you the **Voices that Matter**. But what does that mean? It means that New Riders brings you the Voices that challenge your assumptions, take your talents to the next level, or simply help you better understand the complex technical world we're all navigating.

Visit **www.newriders.com** to find:

▶ *Discounts* on specific book purchases

▶ Never before published chapters

▶ Sample chapters and excerpts

▶ Author bios and interviews

▶ Contests and enter-to-wins

▶ Up-to-date industry event information

▶ Book reviews

▶ Special offers from our friends and partners

  Info on how to join our User Group program

▶ Ways to have your Voice heard

New Riders

WWW.NEWRIDERS.COM

VISIT OUR WEB SITE

WWW.NEWRIDERS.COM

On our web site, you'll find information about our other books, authors, tables of contents, and book errata. You will also find information about book registration and how to purchase our books, both domestically and internationally.

EMAIL US

Contact us at: **nrfeedback@newriders.com**

- If you have comments or questions about this book
- To report errors that you have found in this book
- If you have a book proposal to submit or are interested in writing for New Riders
- If you are an expert in a computer topic or technology and are interested in being a technical editor who reviews manuscripts for technical accuracy

Contact us at: **nreducation@newriders.com**

- If you are an instructor from an educational institution who wants to preview New Riders books for classroom use. Email should include your name, title, school, department, address, phone number, office days/hours, text in use, and enrollment, along with your request for desk/examination copies and/or additional information.

Contact us at: **nrmedia@newriders.com**

- If you are a member of the media who is interested in reviewing copies of New Riders books. Send your name, mailing address, and email address, along with the name of the publication or web site you work for.

BULK PURCHASES/CORPORATE SALES

The publisher offers discounts on this book when ordered in quantity for bulk purchases and special sales. For sales within the U.S., please contact: Corporate and Government Sales (800) 382-3419 or **corpsales@pearsontechgroup.com**. Outside of the U.S., please contact: International Sales (317) 428-3341 or **international@pearsontechgroup.com**.

WRITE TO US

New Riders Publishing
800 East 96th Street, 3rd Floor
Indianapolis, IN 46240

CALL/FAX US

Toll-free (800) 571-5840
If outside U.S. (317) 428-3000
Ask for New Riders
FAX: (317) 428-3280

New Riders

WWW.NEWRIDERS.COM

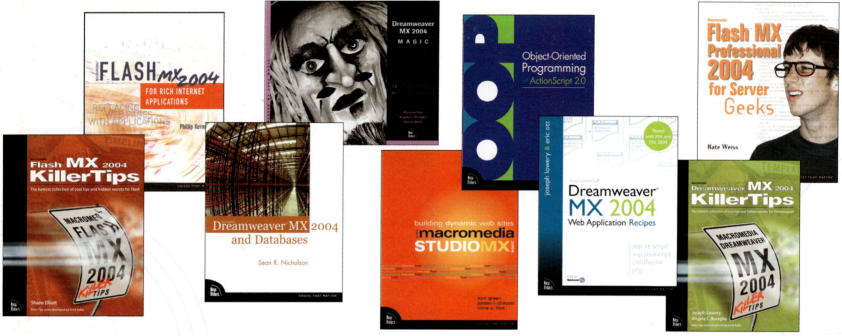

**Macromedia Flash MX 2004
for Rich Internet
Applications**
Phillip Kerman
$45.00, 0735713669

**Macromedia Flash MX 2004
Killer Tips**
Shane Elliot
$39.99, 0735713839

**Macromedia Dreamweaver
MX 2004 Magic**
Massimo Foti,
Angela C. Buraglia, Daniel Short
$29.99, 0735713782

**Macromedia Dreamweaver
MX 2004 and Databases**
Sean R. Nicholson
$45.00, 0735713707

**Building Dynamic Web Sites
with Macromedia Studio
MX 2004**
Tom Green, Jordan L. Chilcott,
and Chris S. Flick
$45.00, 0735713766

**Object-Oriented
Programming
with ActionScript 2.0**
Jeff Tapper, James Talbot,
and Robin Haffner
$45.00, 0735713804

**Macromedia Dreamweaver MX
2004 Web Application Recipes**
Joseph Lowery and Eric Ott
$49.99, 0735713200

**Macromedia Flash MX
Professional 2004 for Server
Geeks**
Nate Weiss
$45.00, 0735713820

**Macromedia Dreamweaver MX
2004 Killer Tips**
Joseph Lowery and Angela C. Buraglia
$39.99, 0735713790

New
Riders

VOICES
THAT MATTER™